GOODNESS IS CONTAGIOUS

From Profit to Purpose

A True Story By David Ash

 FriesenPress

Suite 300 - 990 Fort St
Victoria, BC, Canada, V8V 3K2
www.friesenpress.com

ISBN
978-1-4602-7448-4 (Hardcover)
978-1-4602-7449-1 (Paperback)
978-1-4602-7450-7 (eBook)

1. Religion, Christian Life, Personal Growth

Distributed to the trade by The Ingram Book Company

"David Ash's story is both riveting and moving. *Goodness Is Contagious* is truthful, inspirational, and at times very funny."

—**Dr. David Aikman,** author and former *Time Magazine* Bureau Chief

"Since our meeting in 1998, David has become a great friend and inspiration to our entire family. I have witnessed his personal and spiritual evolution firsthand, and it has changed my life forever. *Goodness Is Contagious,* the story of David's life, is sure to inspire anyone looking for answers to life's most important questions."

—**Nigel Bennett**, co-founder of Aqua-Guard Spill Response Inc.

"This unique and inspiring story will challenge your heart and your paradigms.

If you need to rejuvenate your faith in people, you should read this book.

David is the real thing."

—**Brent Cantelon,** Pastor

"David's walk with God and his testimony altered the path of my life.

What he has to say is worth listening to."

—**Gair Williamson**, architect, Vancouver, BC

Table of Contents

GOODNESS IS CONTAGIOUS

For my father, William Donald "Don" Ash
(1927–1983)

Whose tenderness and unconditional love made
a world of difference to a scared little boy.

Foreword

David Ash, his wonderful wife Lise, and his two adult children, Donavon and Jasmine, are not just acquaintances but dear, dear friends! I've stayed with them in their home a number of times, and I have observed their lives up close and personal in different parts of the world.

This story of David's life journey will not only touch your heart but change your perspective of God's greatness. You will marvel at God's ability to reach down in love to any honest person who is seeking to know Him and lift him up and out, setting him on the road to discover the destiny that God intended from his mother's womb.

David transparently reveals the good, the bad, and the ugly of his life. He unveils mammoth challenges in childhood and youth that he overcame — and yet he did not turn bitter. He helped even the very ones who hurt him the most. It is truly a testimony to the greatness of Jesus in the life of David, his family, his business, and his friends around the world.

When Jesus came into David's life, he became focused on God's goals and purposes and His means and ways to help. With love and listening to the Lord, David began to reach out to those in need and give them a hand up. He lives by principle. He loves deeply and privately does things for others with no desire for acknowledgment. He is a true follower of Jesus.

Just as Paul commended Phoebe to the people of God in Rome (Romans 16:1), I commend David Ash to you. He is a man of God, a person who longs to know Jesus more and more and grow in relationship with Him, a leader and statesman in the area of business, and one who is global in his outlook and outreach. You will be blessed and deeply impacted as you read the story of God at work in the life of David Ash.

Loren Cunningham
Founder, Youth With A Mission
International Chancellor, University of the Nations
Leader, U of N Kona Campus

I bargained with Life for a penny,
And Life would pay no more,
However I begged at evening
When I counted my scanty store;
For Life is a just employer,
He gives you what you ask,
But once you have set the wages,
Why, you must bear the task.

— *Jessie B. Rittenhouse*

Chapter 1
The Moment of Truth

As I surveyed the huge pile of file folders in front of me, my chest tightened. This was the largest financial transaction of my entrepreneurial career. I had started with nothing and risked everything, over and over again, to get here. I was the founder, president, and sole shareholder of a company that employed over 500 people and made millions in profits every year. The business was a virtual money machine.

Sitting at the end of a long mahogany boardroom table on the 35th floor of a downtown skyscraper was my lawyer, David Bentley, a brilliant but cynical man who always seemed a little annoyed. When our eyes finally met, he raised an eyebrow that asked if I really wanted to do this. We both knew that my signature at the bottom of these pages would trigger the irrevocable sale of the most profitable company I had ever owned, and would likely ever own, in my life.

I also knew that many people thought I was crazy to sell, but I didn't care. My mind was made up. I swallowed hard, picked up the pen, and gave David the nod.

Chapter 2
A Rough Start

The 1960s gave us the Rolling Stones, the Beatles, the hippy movement, and the Vietnam War. It was into this turbulent time in history that I was born, on Easter Sunday, April 17, 1960.

School was always a challenge for me. No matter how hard I tried, it seemed I was always getting into trouble. I remember walking home on a sunny June afternoon with a friend. Grade one was finally over, and we were reviewing our report cards. I looked up from mine in confusion. "I failed."

I wasn't so much hurt as perplexed. Why me? Why wasn't I able to succeed?

Failing grade one set the tone for the balance of my educational career. By sixth grade, I'd become so frustrated that I stopped trying altogether. In grade seven, the first year of high school in Quebec, I skipped 264 periods and was threatened with permanent expulsion if I didn't straighten up. My behavior and overall lack of engagement was so serious that the school board had me tested to see if I had a learning disability. I recall the lady examiner looking at me at the end of the test in confusion. "You are perfectly intelligent," she said. "Why aren't you doing your work?"

Arms folded in front of me, I sat in silent, angry defiance. I felt like nothing more than a problem to be managed by the system.

I lived in a rough inner-city neighborhood in Montreal. I hung out with other troubled kids — fighting, stealing, and skipping school. The only thing I was good at was being bad, and I wore it as a badge of honor.

The guys I hung around with were tough and street-smart. My friend Gary's mother had died, and his father was in jail. He lived with his grandmother, a mean-spirited woman who resented having to care for him. She was relentless in her verbal abuse of him, often right in front of me. I can only imagine what went on behind closed doors.

Another one of my best friends was Fanger, who was a legend in our neighborhood. His real name was Andrew, but even his parents called him Fanger. By the age of 10, his use of profanity was both natural and prolific, and there was no secret as to how he'd developed the skill. I'll never forget knocking on his apartment door in the morning and being greeted by his mother, who would begin screaming the most angry, vile profanity at Fanger, telling him to get out of bed, or he'd be late for school again! A few moments later my little friend would emerge sleepy-eyed and oblivious to his mother's tirade, and we would make our way to school, again.

There wasn't anything Fanger wouldn't try to steal. I remember one story of him calmly staggering out of the local IGA store under the weight of a watermelon he could barely wrap his skinny arms around. On another hot summer's day, we were hanging around Phil's, the candy store at the end of our street, which was also the end of the line for city buses. As we walked by two bus drivers who were chatting and having a smoke, we noticed, at our 10-year-olds' eye level, the coin dispensers they wore on their hips. Reading my mind, Fanger reached over, and *click, click!* — two quarters dropped into his hand. We started to run, but the driver spun and caught Fanger with a backhand that sent him sprawling and dropping the coins. Swearing at the driver, Fanger leapt to his feet and continued his getaway.

My friends and I all lived in identical apartments in three-story walk-up buildings. Each unit consisted of three bedrooms, a small living room, a galley kitchen, and one tiny bathroom. My family had three kids, and the space was tight. Fanger had five brothers and sisters, all living in the filthiest little apartment I had ever seen. They were so crowded they had to sleep two to a tiny bed, which was never made and rarely washed.

The challenges I faced in school were compounded by the chaos of my home life. When I was in grade six, my mother had a nervous breakdown, which led to hospitalization in a psychiatric ward for a significant period of time. My father's sister, my aunt Grace, came from Newfoundland to help my dad take care of me and my two brothers (Paul, two years older, and Peter, five years younger). "When I arrived, the house was a mess," Aunt Grace recalls. "The boys were dirty, they all needed haircuts, and they weren't eating properly."

I'll never forget visiting my mother in a psychiatric ward for the first time. Sitting in the waiting area, we noticed the sweetest little old lady shuffling toward us. This darling gray-haired granny, in her cozy nightgown and fuzzy slippers, was looking up at the pictures on the wall, angrily muttering and shaking her head as she passed them. When she came within earshot, her ramblings became clear: Using a creative combination of four-letter words, she was complaining that the pictures on the wall had been stolen from her. Our jaws dropped, and our eyes went wide with confusion and amusement. My brothers and I thought this was hilarious. My mother gave us a reproving look, but even she couldn't suppress a grin as she whispered, "Mrs. Kline has Alzheimer's disease."

A few weeks later, Mum came home heavily sedated on psychiatric medication. This began a rollercoaster ride of emotions for all of us. Our hopes rose as she got better and fell when she crashed. As a teenager, I saw my mother taken away by ambulance more than once after prescription drug overdoses and suicide attempts. These usually happened when Dad was out drinking. With both parents struggling, my brothers and I were forced to pretty much raise ourselves.

As a teenager, I wasn't involved in organized sports or extracurricular activities, except for one: drugs. I discovered drugs in high school, and I got high daily. It was mostly marijuana, which I sold to support my habit and my social life.

By that time, we had moved to a more middle-class suburban area. I suspect this move was an attempt to get me away from my delinquent friends. I had been getting into more serious trouble in the city, stealing and fighting. I was so upset by the move that I almost ran away from home. Hanging out with middle-class kids was a major adjustment for a street tough like me. I was feared and ostracized by the other kids at first. After a year or two, I relaxed somewhat and found friends who were middle-class versions of my city pals, but they were comparatively good kids whose delinquency was limited to recreational drug use.

Chapter 3
The Ride of My Life

When I regained consciousness, I was sitting on the floor of the old muscle car with my feet in the grass. They were sticking out of a hole ripped open by the concrete base of the lamp post we had just hit. The windshield was smashed, with a huge spider web of cracks radiating out from where my head had struck it. A flashlight was shining in my face, and a French policeman was yelling at me. "Get outta da car!"

That's the last thing I remember before I passed out. The next time I woke up, I was in the back of an ambulance.

I was 16 and in grade eleven, the last year of high school. My friends and I had been on our way home from a night on the town, drinking and smoking hashish. Ronny and I were driving our friend Tracy's car, a bright red 1967 Dodge Challenger, because Tracy had been beaten up and arrested by the police two hours earlier. Ronny was thrilled to be behind the wheel of the old muscle car for the first time. Not used to the power and handling, he had accelerated too aggressively into a tight corner and lost control.

I ended up in hospital with four fractures — two in my spine and two in my pelvis — and a concussion. Ronny was unhurt. Two weeks of hospitalization were followed by 30 days of bed rest at home. I had to wear a back brace and walk with canes for another month afterwards. It was by far the most painful experience of my life.

That evening had started like so many others, with the six of us crammed into Tracy's Challenger, laughing and joking as Led Zeppelin pounded over the roar of the engine as we sped down the highway. The laughing stopped when police sirens pierced our music.

Tracy pulled over, but as the officers approached the car, I sensed we were in trouble. Police were never good news, but we had an even bigger concern than the drugs we were carrying: We were English, and the policemen were French. Understanding our position is difficult unless you were in Quebec at the time. Only six years earlier, in 1970, martial law had been declared for the first and only time in Canadian history. This was a response to what became known as the October Crisis. In the early 1960s, a French terrorist group called the Front de Libération du Québec (FLQ) had sprung up in response to the French-speaking majority's concerns over economic, political, and social inequalities. Their stated objective was to separate the Province of Quebec from the rest of Canada.

Now, political tensions between the French- and English-speaking communities in Quebec were still high. Most people were reasonable, but some separatists still hated English people and weren't shy about showing it when they had the opportunity. We crossed our fingers as the police officer approached our car, hoping he wasn't one of them.

The officer and his partner ordered us out of the vehicle and then lined us up, legs spread, hands on the police car. Then the tall, scary-looking cop pulled out his gun and started marching back and forth behind us, screaming and swearing at us in French. We were teenagers who'd been out drinking and smoking dope, not gun-toting criminals. This guy was obviously deranged, and we were terrified.

At that point, Tracy, who had been secured in the back of the police car, leaned into the front seat and opened the passenger door wide enough to stick his head out. "Hey, take it easy. We aren't criminals!"

The policeman spun around and looked at him in shock. Enraged by Tracy's defiance, he kicked the door closed as hard as he could. I heard the crunch of metal against Tracy's face as he fell back into the car. Then the policeman climbed into the passenger seat and began pummeling Tracy, who was trapped in the back seat. His partner soon joined him. Incredibly, all of this had escalated from a routine traffic stop just moments earlier.

When we saw our friend getting beaten up, our adrenaline overcame our fear. We surrounded the police car, yelling and screaming profanities and threatening the cops. We kicked, banged, and jumped on their car, yelling at them to come out so we could kick their asses.

After a few minutes of this, they slammed the cruiser into drive and pulled up the road a safe distance from us. Within minutes, two more police cars showed up, and we watched as the policemen conferred. Then all three police cars turned down a dark side road into an unlit factory parking lot. Fearing for Tracy's safety, we piled into the Challenger and followed.

As we stepped out of our car in the parking lot, six policemen came flying at us, screaming in French and throwing us to the pavement. They yelled warnings and threats, trying to scare us and establish control. Within minutes, they were back in their cars and screeching out of the parking lot with Tracy.

We called Tracy's parents, who rushed to the site of the incident. They quickly decided to go to the police station, and all of my friends who could fit piled into Tracy's parents' car. Ronny and I weren't fast enough to get a seat, so Tracy's father asked if we would drive Tracy's car home. Shortly after that, the accident happened.

When I returned to school six weeks later, wearing a back brace and walking with canes, I was so far behind that graduation, always unlikely, now seemed impossible.

Despite my academic challenges and troubled home life, I'd always had natural confidence. I believed I could make it in the "real world," where I could capitalize on my street smarts. Anxious to start down that road after I recovered from the car accident, I dropped out of high school and moved in with my older brother Paul, who lived three hours away in Ottawa. Free at last, I had a clean slate and a fresh start. I would rise or fall on my own merits, no longer defined by educational challenges, my past, or my dysfunctional family.

Chapter 4
Dreaming Big

As I walked up to the large, dirty, smelly metal sinks on my second day of work as a pot-washer at the YMCA, my heart sank. The sinks were piled high with pots, frying pans, and utensils. I picked up the largest offender — a cast-iron pot covered with concrete-hard spaghetti sauce — and began chipping away, to little effect. I was red-faced and sweating, and the harder I scraped, the more frustrated and humiliated I felt. *I'm better than this,* I screamed inside.

I dropped the pot, ripped off my apron, and told the boss, "I quit." He wasn't happy, but I didn't care. I had a plan: I could sell. I knew I could, because I'd been doing it my entire life.

On the neighborhood streets growing up, my brothers and I were always hustling for a buck. From when I was 12, Paul and I sold newspaper subscriptions door-to-door. After dinner, we would pile into a van with a bunch of other kids, and our crew manager would drop us off all over the city. It wasn't long before Paul and I became the top two producers out of every crew.

Our secret? We developed our own sales system. When a prospect opened the door, we took one full step into the doorway. Inevitably, the person would retreat one step. Then we launched into our impassioned presentation about our "one-week free trial subscription" and how if they took the paper, they would be helping us win a grand prize of some kind. We wouldn't retreat until we heard the word *no* at least three times. It's incredible how many sales we made after the first and second *no*s. That experience taught us that *no* doesn't mean no; it means maybe.

* * * * *

Shortly after leaving the YMCA, I landed a new job at Home Locators, an agency that charged home hunters $25 to access their "exclusive" lists of rental apartments and houses. I worked the phones and the front counter 12 hours a day, six days a week, trying to convince people to use our service. The $200 a week salary wasn't great, but the sales training certainly was.

Part of my job involved dealing with the landlords and real estate agents who listed their vacancies with us. I developed a strong rapport with one real estate agent in particular. As we chatted on the phone one day, I expressed interest in his career. He said he loved the income potential and the freedom it offered. He also thought I'd be good at it. I was flattered and encouraged.

Due to the car accident, I had received a $10,000 insurance claim. At the time, it felt more like $1 million. Either way, it was enough to fund my next adventure. I thanked my friends at Home Locators for everything, signed up for a real estate training course, and moved on.

* * * * *

The real estate licensing program was a university-level course divided into three two-week segments. On the first day of class, I fidgeted as the instructor told my middle-aged classmates and me that a minimum score of 75 percent was required to pass. As I flipped through the huge binder filled with incomprehensible financial and legal jargon, I was terrified. What was I doing here? I had no study skills, self-discipline, or academic confidence. My parents had never even owned a home, and I had no idea what a mortgage was. I realized there were no shortcuts here; the only way out was straight through.

Amazingly, I passed the first segment with a mark of 76 percent. It was too close for comfort, but it was still a pass. On the second segment, by far the hardest, I received 92 percent, one of the highest marks in my class. My confidence soared. I passed the third segment with 85 percent. For most people, passing a real estate course is no great academic achievement, but to me, it felt like I had just earned a PhD. I finally had proof that I wasn't fatally flawed.

After graduation, I got a job with a Century 21 broker owned by an older Austrian gentleman named Alfred, who had a thick German accent. He gave me a desk and a telephone and told me to "gets to vork!" So I gots to vork!

Having been offered very little guidance, for the first two months I basically spun my wheels. Discouraged, I went to Alfred one day and complained that I thought my youthful appearance may be giving some clients a reason to doubt my abilities. "Don't vorry abouts it," Alfred said. "Give ses guy a call. He vill fix you up." It turned out Alfred wore a toupee, and he was setting me up with "his guy." At age 18, I still couldn't grow facial hair, and I was prepared to do whatever it took to succeed.

The next day, as I marched into the office with a full moustache, I was greeted by laughs of encouragement. I was like the company mascot. Everyone wanted to see the new kid succeed. I'll never forget the shocked looks on the faces of clients with whom I had met only days earlier with my hairless, acne-ridden face.

Over the next few days, the glue that held my new mustache in place irritated me, so I began taking it off and putting it on throughout the day, sometimes forgetting it when I met with clients. This turned more than a few heads. It wasn't long before I stashed the 'stache. Thankfully, some real encouragement and direction were right around the corner.

* * * * *

Even though I was surrounded by hundreds of other real estate agents in the luxurious hotel ballroom, I felt like the only person there. The speaker assured us with passion and confidence that no matter who we were, where we were from, or how little education we had, a positive mental attitude could help us achieve great things in life. This was music to my ears. My heart pounded, my mind raced, and the hair on the back of my neck stood up as I tried to process this radical message. For the first time in my life, I was being told that I could achieve great things, and I really believed it.

I hung on every word the speakers uttered that weekend and received them as gospel. I was taught that words and thoughts are "things" and that the thoughts dominating my mind would eventually reproduce themselves in my physical reality. I learned how to set goals and magnetize my mind for success. Finally, I had a clear path out of the poverty and victim mentality that characterized my family's life.

At the age of 18, I set my first major goal: I would be a millionaire by age 30.

Chapter 5
Conquering the World

I left the real estate convention with my arms filled with books and tapes and my mind filled with courage and determination. I read the books, listened to the tapes, and sat up late at night writing out my goals. I went to work each day filled with hopes and dreams of a brighter future.

I was still pretty rough around the edges, but I made up for my lack of knowledge and sophistication with energy and enthusiasm. Wearing my $100 suit, I cold-called day and night. This generated a surprising number of listings and sales for an 18-year-old rookie. It also drew jealous criticism from my veteran peers, who didn't know what a cold-call was.

My confidence level was at an all-time high, and I believed I was destined for greatness. But if I was going to achieve my financial goals, I had to keep moving. In my mind, I'd already conquered the real estate world (even though I had only worked at it for a year). The economy in Ontario had taken a dip, so I moved 2,000 miles away to the booming oil province of Alberta in search of greater opportunities.

* * * * *

Arriving in Calgary broke, I needed to start earning money right away. It wasn't long before I discovered the telemarketing business. It was a commission-only operation, so they were always looking for people to start right away.

Walking into the phone room for the first time was intimidating. The smell of burnt coffee and cigarette smoke filled the air, and the sounds of phones ringing and fifty people talking all at once were deafening. Sitting in cheap stacking chairs and bent over long folding tables, elbow to elbow, with receivers pressed against their ears, people dialed as fast as they could, trying desperately to convince someone to buy what we were selling. Phones slammed and heads shook in frustration while other people smiled and pumped their fists in victory.

Although some detractors called what we ran "boiler rooms," we never did. This derogatory term describes illegal, high-pressure sales operations hidden from authorities in the basements of low-end commercial buildings next to actual boiler rooms. Our offices did look like boiler rooms, and we definitely used high-pressure sales techniques, but the businesses we ran were technically legal.

The telemarketing business attracted some colorful characters. The insider's term for a telemarketer is a *phone man*. Over the phone, we assumed the warm, convincing, and gregarious tones belonging to a middle-management executive. Little did the people on the other end realize they were speaking to a long-haired, unshaven guy in an old Batman t-shirt and ripped jeans whose eyes were glassy from the previous night's drinking. This rogue's gallery of intelligent derelicts, who came from all walks of life, shared two things: an addiction of some kind (drinking, drugs, or gambling) and an inability to hold down a steady job. These street-smart phone men were my people, and I thrived.

I sold advertising and did fundraising. My work ethic and ambition distinguished me from my peers, who had little of either. It wasn't long before I rose through the ranks and was running phone rooms across the country.

As a subcontractor, I essentially had my own business. I rented office space and handled accounts receivables, payables, and payroll. It was a crash course in business ownership and management. Suddenly, at age 22, I was earning more in a week than my father earned in a month. I still needed one thing, though: a new car.

The salesman studied me quietly as I paced around the 1982 collector's edition Corvette like a panther stalking his prey. The sleek, shiny new $32,000 sports car was perfect, a wedding cake on wheels. My adrenaline was pumping. *Can I? Should I?*

Swallowing hard, I gave him the nod.

As I slid into the cockpit and grabbed the padded steering wheel, the smell of new leather filled my nostrils. I drove off the lot that sunny afternoon, engine grumbling at the touch of my toe, windows down, and AC/DC cranked on the stereo. *"I'm on a highway to hell!"*

I felt like a millionaire. I had no idea I was about to run out of gas.

A year later, the company I worked for retroactively altered a deal we had made, costing me $30,000. They had lied to me, and I was furious. I had been a hard-working, honest, and loyal manager. I'd looked up to the people I worked for. They had taught me a lot (in this case, it was the Golden Rule: "He who has the gold makes the rules").

Surprised and hurt by their betrayal, I quit, sold my Corvette at a $10,000 loss, and went backpacking around Europe for the next couple of months.

On the plus side, I was only 22 years old. If phone rooms wouldn't bring me my first million, I would find something that would.

Chapter 6
An Entrepreneur

The Entrepreneur's Credo

I do not choose to be a common man.
It is my right to be uncommon — if I can.
I seek opportunity — not security.
I do not wish to be a kept citizen,
Humbled and dulled by having the
State look after me.
I want to take the calculated risk,
To dream and to build,
To fail and to succeed.
I refuse to barter incentive for a dole;
I prefer the challenges of life
To the guaranteed existence,
The thrill of fulfillment
To the stale calm of Utopia.
I will not trade freedom for beneficence
Nor my dignity for a handout.
I will never cower before any master
Nor bend to any threat.
It is my heritage to stand erect,
Proud and unafraid,

To think and act for myself,
To enjoy the benefit of my creations,
And to face the world boldly and say:
This, with God's help, I have done.
All this is what it means
To be an Entrepreneur.

—*Entrepreneur's Magazine,* 1983
Adapted from "My Creed" by Dean Alfange, 1952

When I read "The Entrepreneur's Credo" for the first time in 1983, it articulated deeply held thoughts and feelings for which I had no words. It spoke to the very essence of my being. My insatiable desire to follow my dreams was neither reckless nor absurd; it was an honorable, dignified, and adventurous pursuit. I finally had a word for what I was: *Yes, my heart cried, I am an entrepreneur!*

Starting with $2,000 in the bank at the age of 23, I struck out on my own. The only question was where to begin. My first idea, which I got from an article in *Entrepreneur's Magazine,* was to promote a career-opportunity exhibition: a trade show that connected job seekers with employers. I booked a convention center, negotiated television advertising, and sold booths. I did all of this from my "corporate headquarters," a single-line telephone sitting on an old children's desk in the unfinished basement of my Edmonton, Alberta, townhouse — and I did it without ever having attended a trade show.

Apart from my lack of experience, I faced one other major challenge: The province was in the midst of a deep recession, and few real employment opportunities existed. I ended up selling booths to whoever would buy them, mostly multi-level marketers and vocational schools. I received more than a few complaints and angry requests for refunds, which I politely declined to grant. Not seeing a profitable future in the exhibition business, I thought it was clear that I would have to make my fortune elsewhere.

My next great idea was the KeepSafe Child ID Kit, which allowed parents to record their children's fingerprints. I built the kits for $4 each and then recruited door-to-door crews to sell them for $15 each. I wholesaled them to distributors as well.

These are just two of the many ideas I brought to life over the next ten years. I ran with some of them for a few months and with others for a few years. Some of them paid the bills, but none of them made me rich. Many other ideas never made it off the drawing board. Eternally optimistic, I loved and believed in every one of them, but my financial realities didn't allow for long-term love affairs that weren't profitable.

My new life as an entrepreneur was a financial version of extreme sports: One wrong move, and I was dead. Living on the edge, I jumped from one great new idea to the next. Sales skills and street smarts were my assets; bookkeeping and accounting, my liabilities. Shoeboxes filled with disorganized check stubs, bank statements, and deposit books piled up. I always paid the bills, but I was often late.

*   *   *   *   *

Compounding the pressures of my new life as an entrepreneur was my father's sudden death in 1983. He died of complications due to diabetes. I actually received the news on a payphone in Italy, where I was traveling while taking a break from the phone business.

Like all young boys, I worshipped the ground my father walked on. As far as I was concerned, he was the strongest and best dad in the neighborhood. I'll never forget how he handled me once in grade four. I had a mean teacher who had no patience for distracted young boys. She smacked me on the back of the head one day for talking to a friend. Fear of this teacher was upsetting me as I struggled with homework one night. Panicked, I finally broke down. My dad asked me what was wrong. I looked up at him with tears streaming down my face. "I can't do the work."

Instead of telling me to work harder or pay attention, like many other parents would have, he patted me on the back and reassured me. "Don't worry about it, David. Just do your best." His tenderness and unconditional love made a world of difference to that scared little boy.

Dad was a blue-collar guy who worked on the loading docks for the railway. He was from Newfoundland, an island floating off Canada's Atlantic coastline. A poor province with a harsh climate and a depressed economy, Newfoundland was a place that people moved away from but rarely to.

"Newfies," as people from that region are called, value family and a sense of humor above all else. True to his heritage, Dad was an encyclopedia of jokes that he told over and over again. My brothers and I would always groan as he teed one up for the hundredth time, but we couldn't resist laughing, because *he* always did. However, his laughter often masked something darker.

After my dad completed grade seven, my grandfather gave him a choice: quit school and go to work or stay and finish his education. The implication was clear: The family needed the money. So at the age of 13, Dad said goodbye to his childhood and signed on at the Matchless Paint Factory. He worked ten hours a day, six days a week, soldering the tops onto paint cans. As he often reminded us, "I made eight dollars a week, gave six home, and kept two for myself." That same year, his mother died. My heart sinks as I imagine him working in those Dickensian conditions after her death.

My father's drinking began in the Navy, where he played bass in the marching band. He was discharged early when he was diagnosed with type 1 diabetes. Like many men, he had joined as a good churchgoing boy but came out a hard-drinking sailor.

Like the Alcoholics Anonymous credo says, "One is too many, and a thousand is never enough." Dad was incapable of having just one drink, which is why he never drank at home. Every now and then — typically after work on a payday — he would disappear, and he wouldn't reappear until the wee hours of the morning, falling down drunk — assuming he wasn't picked up by the police and forced to sleep it off in the drunk tank. When he did make it home, he wasn't mean or angry, but he wasn't happy, either.

In the years after I left home, my father became increasingly sad and bitter. He was living paycheck to paycheck in a small apartment next to the railroad tracks, caring for his mentally ill wife and teenage son, my younger brother Peter.

Things changed two years before he died, though, when he started listening to a radio talk show hosted by a local pastor. Dad started going to church, put on weight, and quit smoking and drinking. He was still broke, and Mum was still sick, but his bitterness and regret were gone.

My father asked me to go to church once. I wasn't a fan of most Christians — I thought many were small-minded and hypocritical — but I wanted to make him happy, so I agreed. I walked into the service that morning very hung over, having had about three hours of sleep. At the end of the service, the pastor gave a passionate explanation of how Christ died for our sins. Then he invited people to come forward to pray. Despite my hangover, I felt an overwhelming compulsion to stand up and walk to the front. However, I doubted the soundness of my mind, so I forced myself to stay put.

I took some comfort in the fact that my father died in peace. I was happy that he was happy. Christianity worked for him, but it made no sense to me. I'd become convinced that to survive in this world, I needed two things: power and wealth.

And Jesus wasn't going to get me either one.

Chapter 7
An Angel in the Lineup

Following my father's death, my little brother Peter, who was 18 at the time, left home for college; my mother, alone now, started going downhill fast. I didn't realize it at the time, but those first few years after Dad died were hard on me, too. My time was divided between working hard during the day and getting high with friends at night. I had no one to talk to, and as always, I used drugs as a coping mechanism.

As a young entrepreneur struggling to survive alone in the world, I had little time or opportunity to reflect on deeper things, like feelings. I just plowed ahead, determined to do whatever it took to "make it happen." All of that changed in 1986 at the Calgary driver's license bureau.

As I stood anxiously in the long line, I groaned. I had no time for this. My attitude changed a few minutes later when a pretty little lady sauntered up behind me with a big, beautiful smile and gorgeous green eyes. We talked non-stop. I asked her if I could show her around town sometime. I'll never forget how she looked up at me, batted those beautiful eyelashes, and smiled. "Oh, really, would you?" she said.

"Oh, yes," I said. "I would."

I left the bureau that day with her number and a promise to call. Lise and I have been together ever since.

The notion that opposites attract was an understatement in our case. If our story were turned into a movie, the tagline would be something like "Tough, street-smart city boy falls in love with sweet, innocent country nurse."

Lise was a French-Canadian Catholic girl from a good family in the tiny French village of St. Anne, Manitoba. Her ancestors had settled the region over a hundred years ago. She came from good, honest, hardworking people who helped their neighbors and respected their elders. She was a straight-A student who volunteered on every committee and flew gliders in the Air Cadets.

As I shared the pain of my past and my dreams for the future, Lise listened with patience and tenderness. She loved my sensitivity and transparency, something absent from her previous relationships. I also think the good girl in her was drawn to the bad boy in me.

In Lise, I saw the love, purity, and stability that had always been missing from my life. She was a woman of uncommon capacity and strength of character, and she still is.

Chapter 8
Render unto Caesar What Is Caesar's

With Lise at my side, my personal life felt more grounded than ever, but on the career front, I was 28 and still constantly dreaming up new ideas, looking for the golden opportunity that would make me a millionaire by age 30. It didn't take long to discover that these new ideas could be both risky and expensive.

Making money wasn't my issue; keeping it was. At the end of each year when tax time came, I had just enough to pay my bills and finance my next great adventure but not quite enough to pay my income taxes. Each year, I thought, *Next year will be different. I'll pay my taxes then.* Six years later, I still hadn't filed a return.

In 1988 Lise and I were living in Toronto because I had expanded my current business there two years earlier. As the pressure mounted, my dreams faded. In my darkest hours, I began to fear that my goals were nothing more than youthful fantasies. Who was I fooling?

I began to see the Tax Man around every corner. To escape the fear and desperation, I got high. When I smoked a joint, my worries would float away, and my bravado would return.

Finally, the dreaded day arrived. I returned to my office after lunch and found a pink phone message on my desk that read, "Mr. Hansen — Revenue Canada Taxation." With trembling hands, I picked up the receiver and dialed. Mr. Hansen was surprisingly polite, not anything like the Nazi I had imagined, but he was firm and very clear: "You have to file your returns, or else . . ."

Four weeks later, I walked into his office, staggering under the weight of three beat-up cardboard boxes crammed with six years' worth of disorganized records and receipts. A few months after that, I received a $125,000 tax bill that I could not pay.

Millionaire at age 30 had become bankruptcy at age 29.

Jumping from one get-rich-quick scheme to another, I had risked everything time and time again. Always swinging for the fences, I had finally struck out. I was bankrupt — mentally, physically, and emotionally. Without any education or formal training, I had nothing to fall back on. It was the lowest point in my young life.

Depressed, I told Lise she deserved better. She should marry a lawyer or a doctor. She was concerned and afraid, but to her credit, she didn't budge.

* * * * *

In the past, my unspoken strategy had been to focus on sales and growth while ignoring accounting and financial planning. It was now clear that if I wanted to succeed, I had to embrace both sides of the equation.

In my search for answers, I remembered a book I had read when I was 18. Written by George Clason in 1926, *The Richest Man in Babylon* has sold millions of copies and is an inspirational classic. Set in the ancient city of Babylon, which Clason describes as "a mixture of grandeur and squalor, of dazzling wealth and direst poverty" (much like many big cities today), the book begins with the story of Bansir, a chariot maker, and

Kobbi, who works as a minstrel. These lifelong friends work long and hard each day but barely earn enough to feed their families. They live in the wealthiest city in the world, but they're trapped in poverty.

Frustrated by this injustice, they struggle to reason their way out of their predicament. Clearly, they're missing something, but what is it? Suddenly, they remember: They know Arkad, the richest man in all of Babylon. They grew up together as equals, playing in the streets and attending the same schools. Arkad's grades were no better than theirs, and yet today, he is "so rich that the king is said to seek his golden aid in affairs of the treasury." What does their friend know that they don't? Arkad kindly receives his friends and their questions and then patiently explains what he has learned and applied so successfully in his life.

As I reread the book, I was drawn in by the simple truth of the parables. Clason makes it clear that success isn't a matter of education or intelligence. It's about knowledge and discipline — knowing what to do and then doing it over and over again *without exception.* Many have the knowledge, but few have the discipline. I was pretty confident I had both.

Another book that was also influential at the time was Napoleon Hill's *Think and Grow Rich.* In the book, Hill essentially explains how to program your subconscious mind for success. One of the key principles is not only writing down your goals but also reading them out loud each day. It felt a little silly at first, but the more I did it, the more success I experienced.

I was young and broke, which meant I had nowhere to go but up. Finally, I had a roadmap, a way out of the mess I was in. But I knew that in addition to knowledge and discipline, success required one more ingredient: teamwork.

Shaken but hopeful, I went to Lise with my head down and *The Richest Man in Babylon* in my hand. Luckily, she saw something in the desperate young man that he didn't see in himself.

"I was a nurse," she now recalls. "I had no interest in being wealthy, but these ideas made sense to me. They promised stability, and that made me feel safe. I saw David commit to us that day and married him in my heart."

Chapter 9
A Fresh Start — Together

Anxious for a fresh start and having no compelling reason to stay in Toronto, Lise and I decided it was time for a change of scenery. As we wound cautiously through the foothills of the Rocky Mountains, just outside of Golden, British Columbia, our wipers struggled to keep up with the snowflakes blanketing our windshield, reducing visibility to a few feet. Our progress was made even slower by the huge homemade trailer dragging the rear end of our Jeep back and forth on the icy road.

When we turned a particularly tight corner, we felt the back end jump. *Bang! Bang! Bang! BANG!* Then nothing. Happy that the Jeep had stabilized, I looked in my rearview mirror, only to discover the trailer was gone.

A few minutes later, I stood with Lise on the side of the road, dancing from toe to toe, shocked and shivering as we looked at our trailer — our life — upside-down in a huge snow bank at the bottom of a deep ditch. I wanted to get back in the Jeep and keep going, but a little voice — Lise! — wouldn't let me. Incredibly, when we finally arrived in Vancouver a few days later and opened the trailer, nothing was broken.

Lise and I were both anxious to get a fresh start in this new city. We rented a little apartment and got jobs. She worked as a nurse for a temp agency, and I went back to what I knew best, running phone rooms.

We took a newfound joy in living frugally and driving beat-up old cars, which I bought for cash, instead of the fancy sports cars I had financed in the past. *The Richest Man in Babylon* and *Think and Grow Rich* had given us a plan, and we were sticking to it.

* * * * *

Two years later, in 1990, I proposed to Lise while on vacation in Mexico. The little resort erupted with excitement at the news.

Three days later, she looked beautiful in the $20 white cotton dress she had purchased from a beach vendor. On our wedding day, we were flanked by my best man, Bob the plumber from Seattle, and Lise's bridesmaid, Jennifer, who happened to be from Vancouver. The service was performed by a glassy-eyed Mexican justice of the peace, who arrived an hour late smelling of tequila. Not one family member from either side was in attendance. It was the most impulsive, unconventional, and romantic wedding I have ever attended. It was totally us.

Nearly two years after our wedding on the beach, Donavon was born. People call childbirth an everyday miracle for good reason. I floated out of the hospital that day shaking my head and thinking, *There has to be a God.* I didn't know who or what he was, but when I looked into my son's face, I knew he had to exist.

By this time, we were also back on our feet financially. We owned a home and had savings, and I was buying and selling fixer-upper houses on the side.

* * * * *

David Ash

Unfortunately, things weren't exactly perfect in paradise. I knew my drug use had played a significant role in my bankruptcy. The tougher things got, the more I used, and the more I used, the tougher things got. So when we'd moved out to Vancouver, I quit cold turkey.

I lasted eight months.

As we got back on our feet, a little voice in my head began to whisper. *Good job. You're back on top. Smoking a couple of joints on the weekend is no big deal. You can handle it . . .* In no time at all, I was back to my old ways, smoking daily and hanging around with people who dealt and used. By most measures, I was a success. But in reality, I had become a high-functioning drug addict. Anyone who says that marijuana isn't addictive is lying or uninformed.

Lise was the first to call me on it. Motherhood fit her like a glove. She was the most loving, nurturing mom in the world. However, after a few months, she made it clear that the drugs and the people who came with them had to go — or else.

She wanted a better future for our child, and so did I. A big part of my desire to succeed in life came from the brokenness of my own childhood. The fullness of my family's life had been stolen by my mother's mental illness and my father's alcoholism. I wanted a better start in life for my son, not a repeat performance.

Chapter 10
The Road to Recovery

I was sitting on a cheap stacking chair in the windowless base-ment of a small church. It was a hot summer's day, and I was elbow-to-elbow with guys wearing black leather, skull rings, and tattoos from knuckles to neck. Thanks to the broken air conditioner sitting on the floor in the corner, the heat was suf-focating. My t-shirt stuck to my chest, and body odor stung my nostrils.

Eventually, a huge biker lumbered to his feet and called the meeting to order. As the room quieted, a wiry little guy flew out of his seat and started yelling and swearing at the 300-pound speaker, accusing him of stealing his tools and demanding their immediate return.

The big biker, shocked by the threats and public accusa-tions, vehemently denied any knowledge of the missing tools or their whereabouts. Accusations and denials flew back and forth. Fists were about to fly when catcalls from the audi-ence demanded that they "take it outside, after the meeting!" Staring hard at the big guy, the accuser slowly retreated, still muttering threats as he took his seat. Instantly the scene returned to normal, causing no more of a stir than a bath-room break.

As I leaned forward, elbows on my knees, unsmiling, I appeared unaffected by the surreal performance. I was very high. I had smoked my last big joint on the way to my first Narcotics Anonymous meeting.

* * * * *

Narcotics Anonymous has the same 12 steps as its big brother, Alcoholics Anonymous.

Step One: "We admitted we were powerless over our addiction, that our lives had become unmanageable."

This step made perfect sense. At age 32, I had been using drugs for over half my life. I couldn't seem to break free from the habit, and I had no problem admitting that I needed help.

Step Two: "We came to believe that a Power greater than ourselves could restore us to sanity."

This was a different matter. The whole idea of God made no sense to me. As a child, I had gone Sunday school, where I'd heard about an all-powerful, all-loving God who cared about me. But those stories were a far cry from my experience, which included my mother being taken away in the ambulance for drug overdoses and suicide attempts while my father went out drinking, leaving my brothers and me to take care of ourselves.

One night during one of these family crises, I lay in bed, crying and cursing God, telling him I hated him for letting these horrible things happen to my family. Despite their failings and struggles, I loved both of my parents. They were good people who loved us. They tried their best, but life had gotten the better of them. So where was God when we needed him? If he was there, I concluded, he didn't care about us. And if he didn't care about us, I certainly didn't care about him.

I discovered that many other new members of Narcotics Anonymous shared my reservations about God, which made the third step all the more challenging.

Step Three: "We made a decision to turn our will and our lives over to the care of God *as we understood Him*."

We were told that we didn't have to define God in any particular way, just as a "higher power." This flexible definition of God is what unlocked the spiritual resistance of members like me who carried religious baggage into the room. "God" could be anything we wanted it to be: Buddha, Jesus, nature, or an energy force.

At its core, Narcotics Anonymous is a spiritual program that takes the addict out of the center of the universe and replaces him or her with a higher power that can supernaturally guide, heal, and console those who surrender to it. The rationale for surrendering to this idea is that "if your very best thinking got you here, what do you have to lose?"

Prayer and meditation are central to the program. The corporate and personal appeal made to this higher power is found in the Serenity Prayer: "God grant me the serenity to accept the things I cannot change, courage to change the things I can, and the wisdom to know the difference." I said this prayer dozens of times a day in the early going, and I felt a lift in my spirit every time I did. Today I believe God heard those desperate prayers, understood my pain, and loved me even though I didn't know or accept him fully yet. You could say Narcotics Anonymous was my spiritual kindergarten.

* * * * *

The importance of these spiritual principles was made crystal clear to me early on. After being clean for a few months, I got a call from my friend Lyle. He had been a heroin addict for several years and wanted to get clean. He heard I was doing well with the NA program and wanted to know how it worked.

I told Lyle about the meetings, the 12 steps, and the NA concept of a higher power. I explained that this higher power didn't have to be defined in any specific way. It could be whatever he wanted it to be. He didn't have to believe in any specific religion. I also told him about the Serenity Prayer. "When I feel like I want to use," I told him, "I say the prayer, and it really helps."

His empty, wooden response haunts me to this day. "Pray? I can't do that."

"You don't have to define God at all," I said.

He gave no explanation. His voice was distant and detached. "I can't do that."

He died from a heroin overdose the next day. God had reached out, but Lyle didn't take his hand.

Thankfully, I did.

* * * * *

With no idea of what to expect and just over 30 days clean, I attended a Narcotics Anonymous convention. It was like an Amway meeting for drug addicts. Hundreds of people had come from all over North America to celebrate and encourage each other in their sobriety.

The celebration of "clean time" is a big part of the NA experience. At the start of the conference, the organizers asked everyone in the audience, starting with people who'd had one day clean, to stand up and be acknowledged. As they stood, they were greeted with enthusiastic cheering and applause from the audience. Then those who had been clean for a week stood up. More applause and cheering. Then it was my turn. Thirty days clean! I stood with tears streaming down my face. I was 32, and I had been smoking dope or using other drugs almost every day of my adult life and for much of my teen years. I knew if I could just stay clean for one year, I could stay clean forever. After I sat down, I looked around the room with admiration and respect for the people with 5, 10, 20, and 30 years clean. As the clean times got longer, the applause and cheering grew louder.

When the celebrations were over, I walked out to an area where they were selling t-shirts and books. I found a t-shirt I liked right away. On the front was a graphic image of clouds with sunlight bursting through. Beneath it were the words "Lost Dreams Awaken." This shirt said it all. Since age 18, I'd had a very clear goal of becoming a millionaire by the time I was 30. I was convinced that financial success would bring me the health, wealth, and happiness I so desperately desired. As the grip of my addiction had tightened, my dreams began to fade. At times it felt as if my past were tapping me on the shoulder and reminding me of who I really was and where I came from — that my dreams were impossible. But in that moment, when I bought that shirt, I received the hope that I needed.

Chapter 11
Every Day Was Payday

By 1994, two years after that Narcotics Anonymous convention, what had seemed impossible was now true. I had two years clean. This was also the same year that my daughter Jasmine was born. My lost dreams had been found again.

It was around this same time that I stumbled upon a business opportunity that would change my life forever. I was the second person in all of Canada to enter the controversial payday loan industry. I had gotten the idea from the first guys, who had offered me an opportunity to invest in their new business. I took a pass on their invitation, but I liked the concept so much that I thought I'd give it a try myself.

Starting with one employee, I rented a 400-square-foot office for $400 per month. It was on the second floor of a rundown two-story building, not far from our home. The first year was filled with the same challenges that all new businesses face, but something happened one Friday afternoon that gave me reason to think I might be onto something special. As I pulled into our parking lot, I saw a small crowd of people standing outside in the rain. They were lined up for something, but what? Squeezing up the narrow stairway and down the hallway, I received suspicious glares from people who assumed I was cutting in. When I opened the door to our little waiting room, I found it filled with customers jostling for a spot at the counter and a chance to apply for one of our loans. Our phones were ringing off the hook, and our anxious staff were processing applications as fast as they could.

Business was booming at Payroll Loans.

* * * * *

A payday loan is a small loan made to someone until his or her next payday. Most customers are sub-prime credit consumers, people who have lost access to conventional sources of credit through banks and credit card companies. Our slogan — "Bad Credit? No Credit? No Problem!" — made our policies very clear: The only thing you needed to qualify for a loan was a job and a bank account. No credit bureau checks were required, which meant an applicant could be in bankruptcy the day he or she applied. All borrowers left a post-dated repayment check for the amount of their loan and our 22 percent fee, dated for their next payday.

Our fees were where the controversy came in. Twenty-two percent for a two-week loan is excessive if you annualize it. In our industry's defense, no one can profitably loan $100 to $500 to potentially bankrupt borrowers at bank interest rates for two weeks, which is why the banks have never done it. A payday loan is not meant to be a long-term solution. It's a financial taxi, and you don't take a taxi from New York to Los Angeles. This logic did little to convince our critics, who considered us loan sharks.

While my skin is thicker than most, I have to admit that the "loan shark" label got tiring after a while. I'd groan inwardly when strangers asked what I did for a living. My answer was either an uncomfortable conversation-stopper or a source of amusement that led to a conspiratorial grin and a chuckle. "Oh, so you're a loan shark," they'd say. I eventually put a stop to this predictable dance by stealing the punch line and introducing myself as a loan shark. Some of the looks I got were hilarious.

By the time I started the company, I'd been in and out of a dozen businesses. I had made a good living at some and struggled with others. I approached every new idea with cautious optimism, but any uncertainty I had about the potential of this new business vanished that Friday afternoon.

Over the next three years, I opened 12 retail outlets across Canada. Getting in early helped a lot. We captured market share quickly and enjoyed healthy profits with little competition. New stores were profitable by year two, so the first stores funded the startup costs and growth of the company in the early years.

Our inventory was cash, which meant, as we grew, we needed more and more of it. Instead of taking on partners, I borrowed money from private lenders at high interest rates. This turned out to be one of the best decisions I ever made, because it allowed me to maintain 100 percent ownership of the company.

*　*　*　*　*

By 1998, the U.S. dollar was trading in the $1.50 Canadian range. This currency differential gave Canadian companies a huge incentive to do business in the U.S. However, the U.S. payday loan industry was ten years older than Canada's, so large companies with hundreds of storefront locations had already gobbled up market share by the time we got there. Our success here would require a new strategy.

Around the exact same time, something of even greater significance was happening: The dot-com boom was on. Experts were heralding in the "new economy." Stock markets were skyrocketing, and kids fresh out of university with nothing more than a business plan were raising millions of dollars for crazy schemes that went nowhere. Venture capitalists and investors were all scrambling for a piece of the next Amazon or eBay, and like every other entrepreneur in the world, I wanted in.

This led us to develop one of the first fully integrated online payday loan services in the United States. Our customers applied for loans over the Internet and received money in their bank accounts electronically the next day. Repayment was withdrawn from those same accounts on payday. Overnight, our small Canadian company had gained access to 300 million American consumers, 24 hours a day, seven days a week.

By 2002, the Internet and the strong U.S. dollar had created a perfect storm of profitability. The small business I had started with one employee had grown to 500 employees processing hundreds of millions of dollars in loans and making millions in profits every year.

At 42, I was the founder, CEO, and sole shareholder of an incredibly successful and rapidly growing company. I answered to no one. Finally, I was the right guy in the right place at the right time. I had arrived.

* * * * *

As I sat in my large corner office one sunny afternoon in 2002, I looked out my window and thought, *What next?*

Success had brought an enormous sense of accomplishment and a new life filled with incredible options. We lived in a beautiful home, took five-star vacations, traveled first class, and helped friends and family in need. So why was I filled with doubts and mixed emotions?

Explosive growth had created financial and operational complexities that were new to me. As a result, I was forced to surround myself with new highly paid employees, consultants, and advisors. Suddenly, my jokes were funnier, and I was more popular than ever before. Fewer and fewer people could relate to the reality of my new life. My brothers Peter and Paul had joined the company, and I trusted them completely, but beyond that, agenda-free relationships were almost impossible to find. I was discovering that isolation was a part of the price you pay for extraordinary success.

I was trapped between two worlds — no longer belonging in the world I was from and an imposter in the world I was in. My life felt like a jigsaw puzzle with a big piece missing right in the middle.

During this period of uncertainty, my greatest source of encouragement and support came from my membership in my EO Forum Group. The Entrepreneurs Organization is a peer-to-peer group of entrepreneurs from around the world that is broken down into local chapters. Chapters are further divided into Forum groups of 10 to 12 members who act as an informal board of advisors for each other. Confidentiality — a cornerstone of Forum membership — is a critical element of its success. It gives entrepreneurs a safe place to share their most challenging business, personal, and financial issues. This transparency builds deep personal friendships that last a lifetime.

In addition to hosting international conferences, EO sponsored the Birthing of Giants program, of which Michael Dell, founder of Dell computers, was a graduate. Once a year, 60 of us came together on the beautiful MIT campus in Boston for four days. Through exploring case studies, listening to expert speakers, and sharing our experiences, we learned how to fast-track the growth of our already successful companies.

As I settled into my seat one afternoon, our instructor told us to take a few moments and reflect on the mentors who had shaped our lives most and why. While surveying my bright, college-educated peers with their heads down, scribbling away, I was made painfully aware of how different my life really was. I stared at the blank piece of paper in front of me. I had no one.

Chapter 12
A True Warrior

The last time I saw my mother alive was in Edmonton in 1996. I was looking for office space for my growing payday-loan company. As I drove my rental car through a busy intersection, I caught a glimpse of someone who looked familiar. I glanced again and saw a rough-looking elderly woman waiting to cross the street. *Could it be?*

Yes! It was Mum. I'd had no idea she was in Alberta, let alone Edmonton. The last time I had spoken with her, she had called from Winnipeg or Montreal and was pushing another one of her conspiracy theories. Normally, I didn't try too hard to refute her, but that time I questioned her, and she got upset and hung up on me. I hadn't heard from her since.

I pulled over quickly. With my heart pounding and my mind racing, I followed her into a bus depot restaurant. I watched her from a distance as I composed myself. The disheveled bag lady in front of me, walking with a pronounced limp, was a ghost of the woman I had known and loved. Her hair was dirty, her false teeth were gone, and her clothes were old, smelly, and dirty, but it was her.

"Hey, Mum. How you doing?"

She looked up, startled, cool, and suspicious. "What are you doing here?" Those were her first words to me in two years.

"I'm in town looking for some office space."

After a few minutes, she relaxed and began talking freely. We ate and then went back to her tiny room in a low-end hotel across from the bus depot.

I received the usual rambling update on her long list of imaginary medical conditions and conspiracy theories. By this time, her grandchildren, Donavon and Jasmine, were 5 and 2. She didn't ask a single question about them, me, or Lise. She was completely self-obsessed.

At the end of our time together, I emptied my pockets of the few hundred dollars I had and gave it to her in exchange for a promise to stay in touch. As I walked out of her dumpy little room, tears filled my eyes, and I burned with anger, frustration, and guilt. Every attempt we had made to help her had failed. There was nothing I could do to save her. The beautiful young woman of my youth, my mother, was gone forever.

* * * * *

"Woman dies alone in rooming house," screamed the headline of the Halifax tabloid.

A slumlord had found my mother's body on July 1, 1999 while looking for his overdue rent. The last confirmed contact anyone had had with her was an emergency room visit on June 21, ten days earlier. Determining an exact cause and time of death by that point was impossible. The article indicated there were "no known next of kin." By the time word of her death reached my brothers and me, the funeral had been held, and my mother had been buried in a pauper's grave.

* * * * *

When she was healthy, my mother was a force to be reckoned with — a larger-than-life character whose presence filled the room. She was bold, charismatic, audacious, street-smart, manipulative, and exasperating, right to the end. You might not have liked her, but you couldn't ignore her.

Growing up as an orphan in Montreal's slums made her a fighter in every sense of the word. She was born to a Depression-era prostitute, and social services took her away from her mother at age 2. The fact she had been born with syphilis made her unadoptable, so she became a permanent ward of the court.

Foster parenting in those days wasn't what it is today. Many people took in children for cheap labor or additional income. She was bounced from home to home, where she suffered sexual and physical abuse at the hands of some of her "parents."

Her luck changed at age 14, when an affluent family took her in. They were good people who needed help with their four daughters and mentally handicapped son. Over time, she became part of the family. By the time she was 20, they adopted her as their own.

Despite the kindness shown to her in her late teens, growing up as a ward of the court gave my mother a distorted set of parenting skills. One year, she applied for several Christmas hampers. I remember her coaching my brothers and me not to say anything about what we were getting for Christmas. Then, when the doorbell rang, we stood at attention to receive our kind visitors. With rosy cheeks, dripping noses, and a dusting of snow on their shoulders, they smiled sympathetically while juggling armloads of gifts. After much head-patting and the exchange of many "Merry Christmases," our generous guests left. As soon as the door closed, we flew into action like a NASCAR pit crew, hustling the packages into hiding. An hour later, the sound of the doorbell signaled that another round was about to begin. Exciting stuff for three little boys at Christmas. We didn't *need* one hamper, let alone three. But like all mothers, she wanted the very best for her children. Right or wrong, this was her way of getting it.

What Mum lacked in basic nurturing skills, she made up for in other ways. My brothers Paul and Peter have albinism, a genetic condition that results in the absence of pigment. Their skin and hair are pure white, and both of them are legally blind. Their poor vision made sports and reading blackboards impossible. Unfortunately, 50 years ago, public schools did little to accommodate children with special needs. Frustrated by the lack of help for Paul, Mum cofounded a nonprofit group, Quebec Aid for the Partially Sighted (QAPS). As a result of their advocacy, some visual and teachers' aides were in place by the time Peter made it to school.

My mother's fierce loyalty extended to me as well. Whether I was fighting at school or getting into trouble on the streets, she always gave me the benefit of the doubt. She was also my biggest fan. I remember Mum, when she was well, attending my football games and screaming, "Go, David, go!" as I ran for a touchdown.

* * * * *

My father's sudden death in 1983 left my mother alone. With the only sane anchor in her life gone, she declined quickly. Periods of extreme mania were marked by desperate calls to my brothers and me at all hours of the day and night, recounting wild conspiracy theories. Her aggressive, manic nature brought her into regular conflict with health authorities, landlords, neighbors, and police. She burned bridges wherever she went.

When my father died, I was 23 and constantly on the move chasing my dreams, and my brothers were in university. They tried to support her, as they lived in the same community, but her obsessive, erratic behavior became all-consuming.

To preserve their sanity and their personal lives, they had to establish communication boundaries. I stayed in touch with my mother a little longer over the phone and gave what financial support I could, until one day she stopped calling altogether. Over the years, she drifted unrestrained into her own increasingly delusional world.

She became highly mobile, moving from city to city without rhyme or reason. At first, she lived in rental apartments, but the stability necessary to maintain this type of housing was beyond her. Her homes became rooming houses, emergency shelters, psychiatric wards, and sometimes, jail.

One of her many run-ins with the authorities is a matter of public record. The front-page headline of the April 3, 1992 issue of the *Calgary Herald* read, "Only jail had bed for Vivian." Two follow-up stories on April 4 and May 2 were titled "Mentally ill fall through cracks" and "System can't find a place for homeless woman." She was arrested initially on March 25, 1992 for "causing a disturbance." The events leading up to the charge occurred after she was evicted from an apartment complex for elderly and handicapped people. With nowhere else to go, she went to a hospital emergency room, hoping to get admitted for psychiatric care. When they refused to admit her, she began screaming and yelling at the staff, refusing to leave. This led to her arrest.

Mum spent a week in jail awaiting a hearing on the charge and, during that time, was assessed by a psychiatrist as "mentally fit." (The doctor's diagnosis leads me to believe that he may have needed more help than she did.)

The news report stated that "[Vivian] Ash is intelligent and articulate, but has been labeled manipulative, disruptive and a hypochondriac. She says she is legally blind, has seven ulcers, suffers from emphysema and is recovering from a heart attack and stroke." We discovered later that she supported her legally blind claim by intentionally failing an eye exam and obtaining a card from the Canadian National Institute for the Blind.

The report quoted the Crown prosecutor as saying, "Dozens of professionals from social agencies and the medical community have attempted to help Ash but found there is nothing they can do for her." Another article states, "Ash is said to have burned her bridges with dozens of social agencies, homes and hospitals."

When the case first came to court, the judge was clearly concerned with her well-being, saying it was "a shame that someone can't find a place to put her" and asking, "Isn't there some way we can help her?" She was willing to plead guilty and told the judge that she would "walk out of this building and sleep on the street." However, the judge said this possibility raised "concerns about her safety."

Despite the psychiatrist's determination, the judge ordered her to be reassessed. The next day (April 4, 1992), "she was ordered to undergo a 30-day psychiatric evaluation." According to the *Herald,* "Ash gave a wide smile as she was led away to the General Hospital's forensic unit — a guaranteed bed and three meals per day." Exactly what she wanted in the first place.

On May 1, she was declared mentally fit to stand trial. She pleaded guilty to the charge of causing a disturbance and was sentenced to time served in custody. By late Friday, she was back on the streets, though no one knew where she would go.

* * * * *

As soon as my brothers and I heard about my mother's death, we flew to Halifax. The moment we checked into our hotel, we walked into a firestorm of media coverage. Our sudden appearance gave new life to a sad story that had almost run its course. Soon, we found ourselves on the phone with reporters filling in the details of my mother's life.

Later, we discovered that the intense local media coverage surrounding Mum's death was the work of a wonderful man named Juan Carlos Canales. He was managing editor of *Street Feat: The Voice of the Poor*, an anti-poverty publication supported by local advertisers. Instead of panhandling, homeless and underemployed people sold *Street Feat* on city corners to passers-by.

Juan Carlos gave my brothers and me a valuable glimpse into Mum's world and her last days on earth. He called her a friend and told us that she was known for her temper and stubbornness but that she was also gentle and forgiving. "We called her 'The Warrior Vendor,' " he said. "She was the most dedicated vendor we had."

Our most surprising discovery was her creative talent. Juan Carlos said she wrote poems and articles for the paper, which many readers commented on and enjoyed.

Mum's memorial service was held at a church that ran a weekly dinner for the homeless. As we approached the building, I felt frozen with fear. I didn't want to go inside. I had spent my entire adult life running as hard as I could away from the sadness of my family's life and my mother's reality. I couldn't look into the face of poverty and homelessness without feeling completely broken. Years of unresolved emotions that had been bottled up felt dangerously close to the surface.

As I entered the building, I felt as if I were entering another dimension. The stacking chairs were filled with street people and volunteers who ran the dinner. My brothers and I sat with Mum's adoptive mother and sisters. They were the ones who had raised the alarm after reading an obituary in the Halifax paper about a woman who had died alone. They became suspicious when the names in the obituary were a combination of her birth and maiden names. This was not surprising, given her prolific use of aliases over the years.

As the service began, Ann, a volunteer, welcomed everyone. She introduced us and then, after kind words of remembrance and a prayer, invited anyone who wanted to say a few words to come up to the mike. I was surprised and deeply touched as a friend of Mum's from the street, an aboriginal woman, spoke glowingly of her and the friendship they had. "Vivian had it rough, but she was always there for you. She was a good friend." This lady's feelings of love and loss were clear. She knew and cared for my mum when I couldn't. In that moment, my heart shifted.

Paul was the first family member to take the mike. The least emotive of the three brothers, he quickly broke down into tears. "She was a good mother," he said. "She did the best she could with what she had. She never had a fair chance at life." We were all emotional basket cases after that. Through our tears, Peter and I shared similar sentiments with this roomful of strangers.

Afterwards I had a nice chat with Ann, who I discovered was actually "Doctor" Ann Mott. "I liked your mum," she said. "She was quite a character. We were good friends. She would get mad at me sometimes, but she was always quick to forgive and forget."

I learned later that this humble woman who called my mother a friend wasn't just a doctor; she was one of Nova Scotia's preeminent ophthalmologists. I had always thought doctors hung out at country clubs, not homeless missions. I hadn't met anyone like Ann before. Apparently, she was a Christian.

David Ash

Chapter 13
A Force for Good

A few years after my mother's death in 1999, as I returned to what would be my final year in my Birthing of Giants class sponsored by the Entrepreneur's Organization, I reflected on all I had overcome to get there. Despite my lack of solid mentors, my persistence and determination had paid off. After overcoming my addiction, I had found the business that would change my life. I was proof positive that no matter who you were, where you were from, or how little education you had, you could overcome the challenges of your past and achieve great things. I had bought what the motivational speakers were selling, and it paid off far better than I had ever dreamed. I had my health, financial independence, and a beautiful family who loved me. I was the Canadian version of the American Dream. So why did I feel like something was missing?

The topic that afternoon was "Using your business as a force for good." Two classmates were invited to share their personal experiences. One of them told a story about his auto parts manufacturing business that caught me completely off guard.

Mike was an engineer with a very serious, thoughtful, and pragmatic demeanor. There was nothing flashy or verbose about him. As the facilitator asked him questions, Mike would pause, measuring the truth and efficiency of his words, and then reply in the deliberate manner you'd expect from an engineer. He quietly explained how his company gave away 20 percent of its profits, right off the top, to help poor and needy people around the world.

Twenty percent? I thought. *That's incredible!* I had been working and risking everything I had throughout my adult life to build a company that actually generated a profit, and here he was giving 20 percent of his profits away. Mike went on to explain that the company extended this same generosity to employees, sharing 25 percent of company profits with them and giving them two extra weeks of paid holiday each year as long as they used it to give back in some way. Unlike some companies that used their giving as a marketing tool, Mike's company made no public mention of its benevolent activities. Our class was a rare exception.

Nobody's that generous, I thought. *There has to be a catch.* I had to know more, so after dinner that night, I sat down with Mike one-on-one. As tactfully as I could, I dug deeper, looking for ulterior motives, cracks in his story. Except for Mother Theresa and maybe Gandhi, I believed that great acts of kindness and generosity were never what they seemed. There was always a hidden agenda or angle of some kind. My cynical nature made it difficult to believe that any charitable organization was honest or effective.

Mike responded to my questions in a quiet, humble way, completely unimpressed by his own generosity. At one point, perplexed by my keen interest — and perhaps by my cynicism — he paused and studied me. "This isn't unusual for us," he said. "It's just how we were raised. I'm a Christian. My grandparents didn't have much. Granddad was a janitor at the local college. I remember as a boy visiting my Grandma in their small mobile home and watching her line up five- and ten-dollar checks on a folding card table in her living room. She would smile, and her eyes would light up as she spoke about the wonderful people they were helping all over the world. They took great joy in giving, and they passed that on to us."

I had always relied heavily on my street smarts, and they told me Mike was telling the truth. As the saying goes, "If you want to know where someone's heart is, find their wallet." I knew where his was. It challenged me in a way I had never been challenged before. His life of benevolence was a million miles away from my reality. Mike was a good, honest, down-to-earth guy from a Christian home. This life fit him. I was a loan shark, a tough inner-city guy from a screwed up family from the wrong side of the tracks. If I followed Mike's example, what would people think?

The next morning, when the private car service picked me up for my trip to the airport, I settled into the comfort-able leather seats in the back of the elegant black sedan and enjoyed the subtle jazz music as we wound our way through the MIT campus. The charming heritage buildings, perched on the large lawns dotted with colorful oak and maple trees, had a dreamlike quality to them. It *was* a dream, a dream come true.

As a kid growing up in low-income housing on the west end of Montreal, only blocks away from Concordia University, we often saw fresh-faced young men and women walking and laughing, books in hand, around a very similar campus. They looked so perfect and carefree with their clean Levi's jeans, white runners, neatly cut hair, and bright white smiles. I imagined they all came from happy, affluent families in the suburbs somewhere. Now I was on a similar campus. I wasn't going to school, but I had earned my way there in other ways. It should have felt perfect, but it didn't.

As I reflected on my time with Mike the previous evening, whispers of doubt swirled with a new excitement and a hope that I had finally found a way to make sense of the new life I had.

Chapter 14

Street Mom

"Street Mom needs a home," read the front-page headline over the picture of an unhappy looking, rumpled elderly lady sitting on a medical scooter. The article went on to explain that Ellen Shonsta, a.k.a. Street Mom, had earned her name on the streets of Vancouver, where she was known as "Mom" to several homeless teenagers.

A former foster parent to over 70 children, Ellen was alarmed by the number of kids she saw living on the streets of Vancouver. "I just started feeding them sandwiches, drinks, vitamins, apples, whatever I could find," she said in the article. "It started with 30 or 40 people but grew quickly. In no time, I was feeding 700 people a day." The article was an appeal for help. The church kitchen located on her route was no longer available, and she had two weeks to find a new place to make her sandwiches and store her food.

My mother's life and death had given me a window into the lives of the mentally ill and homeless, and it wasn't pretty. Mike's story had inspired me to get out of my comfort zone and make a difference in my community, but I didn't know where to start. Maybe this was it. Not knowing where else to turn but wanting to help out somehow, I picked up the phone and called the reporter who had written the story.

Things happened fast from there; they had to. With only two weeks left, time was running out. After a brief meeting with Ellen, I agreed to help. She found a nice two-bedroom apartment on her route, and I paid the first and last months' rent and moving costs. Street Mom had a new home.

After she settled in, I dropped by for a visit. The older three-story walk-up apartment building was located on a nice tree-lined street in downtown Vancouver. As the door to her little apartment opened, I was taken aback. None of the creature comforts you'd expect in an elderly woman's apartment were visible: No tidy living room with three generations' worth of family photos displayed proudly on coffee tables. No cute little tea doilies or a pampered cat called Whiskers. Instead, I walked into what amounted to a commercial kitchen storage room. I weaved my way carefully around boxes of clothes and crates of food piled haphazardly. Homemade shelves lined the walls from floor to ceiling, jammed with large cans and boxes.

And then there was the proprietor herself. Ellen was a straight-talking lady who stood at 5 feet, 2 inches and weighed more than she should. Severe, degenerative arthritis made mobility painful and difficult, but she never complained. She spent her days preparing for the night ahead. Then, at around 10:00 p.m., rain or shine, she hit the streets.

As she rolled around on her scooter, pulling a small trailer full of sandwiches, soup, energy bars, blankets, and socks, rough-looking teenagers with multicolored hair, piercings, and tattoos would appear magically from doorways and alley-ways, greeting her with hugs and cries of "Mom!" Ellen fed, clothed, and encouraged every one of them, admonishing her kids to be safe.

"Nothing makes me happier than helping these kids," she said, and she took no credit for the work she did. "I have nothing. I'm a pensioner. I pray, I trust God, and he always provides."

I asked her about the kids she helped. "Most people don't understand," she said. "They think these kids are just bad. They don't realize that some of them are safer on the streets than they are at home. The stories I hear would break your heart." She explained that it's not her job to judge these kids, just to love them. She said the Bible is very clear on this. "As Christians, we are supposed to feed the hungry, clothe the naked, and care for the widows and orphans. I'm just trying to do that."

As we talked, I looked out onto the first floor balcony and noticed a freezer. When I saw that it wasn't locked, I expressed concern about someone climbing up and stealing food. Ellen gave me a puzzled look, as if she were teaching a child. "Why would I worry about someone taking food? If they are taking it, obviously they need it."

I was speechless.

Chapter 15
A Housekeeper's Prayer

As I walked nervously into the large, brightly lit church sanctuary with my neighbor Andrew, the father of one of Jasmine's playmates, I assured myself that I was only there to check things out for the kids. I wasn't a Christian. I thought God might exist, but I didn't think he was knowable or that he had anything to do with our lives.

Andrew and I had become friends in a neighborly sort of way. He stood 6 feet, 6 inches tall and had a personality to match. An extreme sports enthusiast, pilot, and motocross competitor, he was also a Christian. The common ground that brought us together was business. He owned a chain of cellular telephone stores.

Being in a church for the first time in over 20 years was nowhere as unusual as the circumstances that had brought me there. I have epilepsy, which I have dealt with since my early 20s. Under normal circumstances, it's controlled by medication, but my new neurologist had recommended a change in drug treatment, which triggered a random grand mal seizure. A grand mal, as opposed to a petit mal, is the most intense type of seizure there is. Your eyes roll back in your head. You make guttural moaning sounds, experience total body spasms, and then collapse unconscious. I imagine the effect is similar to what happens to your body if you're electrocuted.

The most embarrassing experience I ever had as a result of this affliction had occurred a few years earlier on a business trip. My long flight into Montreal had been delayed. When I finally arrived, I discovered my bags had been lost. By the time I checked into my hotel at 1:00 in the morning, I was completely stressed out and exhausted. I crawled into bed, called down for a wake-up call at 6:00 a.m., closed my eyes, and passed out.

The next, and only, thing I remember before coming to again is the piercing ring of the wake-up call. When I eventually regained consciousness, I was slumped over a large ottoman chair in my hotel room, buck naked. I felt as if I'd been hit upside the head with a cast-iron frying pan. For some reason, a very large and very angry man wearing a dark suit and carrying a walkie-talkie was yelling at me. "Sit down, and don't move!" he said.

Perplexed at the surreal scene and unable to speak, I stared blankly at the man until my brain unscrambled enough to form a sentence. "Why are you yelling at me?"

The man jumped back, startled. "You were walking around naked, two floors down. I found you standing in front of the elevators pushing the buttons. You can't do that!"

As he spoke, my head finally cleared enough for me to realize what had happened. I apologized and told him I was an epileptic and that I must have had a seizure. He had found me in a postictal state, a semi-conscious period right after a seizure when the lights are on but nobody's home. It can last anywhere from five to twenty minutes.

Still upset, he told me to take my medication and then left the room. Later, with my clothes on, I found him in the lobby and thanked him for getting me back to my room.

Now, my most recent seizure had taken place at home. Our housekeeper Bonnie missed the actual seizure but saw me a few moments later in a postictal state. She had been our housekeeper for over three years and had become close with Lise and the kids. Her daughter was Jasmine's age, and the two girls had become friends. Bonnie was a soft-spoken Christian lady with an authentic and gentle spirit, and when she saw me in this condition, she was quite distressed. (Thankfully, I'd had my clothes on, or she would have been *really* upset.)

Apparently, when she went home that night, she prayed for me. The next day, she called Lise and told her that while she was praying, God had spoken to her. "God told me to pray *with* David."

When it came to the subject of God, I was still angry and bitter. I also resented pious and phony Christians who spouted simplistic slogans about God's love, grace, and mercy while having never experienced any real hardship. However, I did admire true followers who lived out their faith with integrity — people like Street Mom and Bonnie, who expressed a love for others that was not contrived. Such people didn't make me feel like a sinner who needed to be saved from the flames of hell, just a neighbor who needed to be loved.

Knowing how cynical I was, Lise approached me cautiously the next day with the news. The idea startled me. *Is Bonnie hearing voices?* I wondered. The request sounded odd, but I was touched by her concern, and I didn't want to offend her. Out of respect, I agreed to meet. What could it hurt?

The next day, we sat down in the living room for a chat. After a short while, Bonnie asked if she could pray for me, and I agreed. As we closed our eyes and bowed our heads, she began by thanking God for bringing her and our family together. Then she made a direct appeal on my behalf, asking God to heal me of my epilepsy. As she prayed, her voice cracked, and she began to cry. I had never had someone

I barely knew care enough to pray for me and cry for me. Tears filled my eyes. I didn't know what to say or do. After she was done praying, for some strange reason I asked about her church.

The following day, Lise and the kids were leaving for a two-week visit with her family. I would be home alone for the next three weekends. I told Bonnie that since I would have all this time on my hands, I might check out her church — for the sake of the kids, of course. Lise and I both believed in "Christian values," and we had discussed the idea of sending the kids to Sunday school. We thought it would be good for them.

That was how I found myself standing in a Pentecostal church the following day with Andrew, who attended the same church as Bonnie. I had never seen anything like it. The large, modern sanctuary held over 2,000 people. The beautiful building, with its large stage and state-of-the-art sound system, was in stark contrast to the smaller, more somber hymn-singing church I had attended as a child.

Nervously avoiding eye contact with anyone — apart from Bonnie, who gave me a smile from across the room — I watched as people laughed and greeted one another. By the time the service began, I was having serious doubts about my decision to attend.

After a short series of announcements, the worship team, which looked more like a rock band, began to play. The musicians, the sound system, and the auditorium were as professional as anything I had seen before. As music filled the air, people raised their hands and sang. Others closed their eyes in prayer.

Suddenly, I was overwhelmed with emotion. As I stared at the floor with my faced screwed up tight, tears filled my eyes. The harder I fought, the more I cried. I felt like everyone in the church was looking at me. I'm sure Andrew didn't know how to respond. I couldn't control myself. It made no sense.

Thankfully, the music finally stopped. I grabbed some Kleenex from a nearby box to blow my nose and wipe my eyes. I resolved to keep my act together until the end of the service. Then I would go home and figure this out.

A few minutes later, the pastor got up and began his sermon. As I listened, tears filled my eyes again. I cried throughout his entire message. The tears had nothing to do with anything he said. There were no amazing revelations or spiritual insights, just an energy in the air.

With Lise and the kids out of town, I had lots of time to reflect on what had happened that Sunday. True, I was going through a bit of a mid-life crisis. Success didn't satisfy me like I'd thought it would. On top of that was my recent seizure, which had taken a lot out of me — post-seizure, you feel as if you've run a marathon you didn't train for. I was mentally and physically exhausted. In this weakened state, I concluded, I had simply gotten caught off-guard and swept away. To prove my theory, I decided to return the following week to objectively evaluate what had occurred and why.

The following Sunday, Andrew accompanied me to church once again. This time, I resolved to maintain my composure no matter what. As we took our seats, I surveyed the congregants suspiciously. *These affluent suburbanites don't know where I come from and don't care,* I thought. *They were probably raised in the church and figure guys like me are going to hell.*

The service began the same way as it had the previous Sunday with greetings and announcements. I stood up straight, shoulders back, clear-minded and ready to assess the situation.

The worship team was introduced and began to play. The high-energy music filled the air. On cue, the people closed their eyes and raised their hands. While some sang and others prayed, I began to cry — again. This time, I was swept away in a tsunami of emotion with sobs so intense they felt as if they were coming from the very core of my being. The harder I fought for control, the more I cried, right to the end of the service.

What was happening to me?

Chapter 16
Surrender

The only reference point I had for my spiritual experience was my father's conversion 20 years earlier. I had come home for Christmas that year. My parents and my younger brother Peter were living in a tiny, two-bedroom apartment on the second floor of a three-story walk-up next to the railroad tracks. As I stepped into the kitchen, Dad was sitting where he always sat with his skinny legs crossed and a big mug of hot tea in front of him. As soon as he saw me, he jumped out of his seat with a huge smile on his face and gave me a hug. "Welcome home, David!" he said.

When he sat down again, he was still smiling ear to ear. He had put on weight and looked healthier than I had ever seen him. I'd heard he had even quit drinking and smoking. As an insulin-dependent diabetic, he shouldn't have been doing either. Next to his mug of tea was something I had never seen before: a large, well-worn Bible.

He was still broke and working on a loading dock in the train yards. Mum was still sick in bed, comatose on psychiatric medications either at home or in the psych ward, but his bitterness and regret were gone.

Back in the days when Dad came home drunk, he'd sing Newfie jigs, which are similar to Irish ballads. "This is the place where the fisherman gather!" he'd sing in his deep baritone voice. Now, I watched in wonder as the same man sang a completely different song — "Amazing grace! How sweet the sound that saved a wretch like me!" — as tears ran unashamedly down his face. For the first time in my life, I could see he was truly happy and at peace. I didn't understand his spiritual experience, but I was happy he had it. Peter told me that he often saw Dad on his knees in the living room, praying and crying out to God, asking for the salvation of his sons. Little did I realize that Peter and Paul would follow in my father's footsteps a short time later.

Witnessing Dad's transformation firsthand also marked me in ways I didn't realize at first. When I was in a tight spot and life wasn't making sense, I'd often reflect on my father's experience and secretly wonder, *Is it true?*

* * * * *

By the third Sunday at church, I felt like I was stuck on a ride and couldn't get off. I was being swept up and consumed by the spirit of this church. By that point, much of my resistance was gone. I was saying, "God, I think you're there, but I just don't understand."

As the music began, the now-familiar waves of emotion overwhelmed me, and I began to cry once again. At the end of the service, Bonnie conferred briefly with Andrew and then asked if I'd like to pray. At that point, I didn't know what else to do, so I agreed.

Don, an elderly pastor, joined us in a small prayer room behind the sanctuary. He asked if I knew what it meant to give my life to Christ. I'd been crying and blowing my nose so much that all I could do was nod. He asked me to kneel down and then explained the relevance of a prayer that invited God into my life. "When you surrender your life to Christ and ask

God for forgiveness for all of your sins," Don said, "he comes into your life and takes it over. You are born again, washed clean and perfect like a newborn baby."

I gasped the prayer through my sobs, with tears running unashamedly down my face, and it made no sense. But I knew in the deepest part of my soul that it was true — I was that baby, washed clean and perfect in the love of Christ. I felt the presence of a supernatural love, like a heavy, wet, warm blanket. It took my breath away.

My sinful life flashed before my eyes. I had been greedy, dishonest, immoral, and very angry. I saw myself alone in bed at night as a child with tears streaming down my face, cursing God and telling him that if he was there, I hated him. I was so sorry for being angry with him. I felt dirty, unworthy, and unforgiveable. My utter shame and disappointment collided head-on with God's pure and perfect love, his amazing grace.

The next day, Lise came home with the kids. They were excited to be back and were bursting with news of the great time they'd at the Festival du Voyageur, a winter festival that celebrates the historical and cultural roots of Lise's French-Canadian ancestors, who settled Manitoba. After we got caught up, Lise turned to me and asked, "How are you?"

As I sat there looking at her, still emotionally drained, I struggled to put my experiences into words. Finally, I looked at the floor and mumbled, "I'm a Christian!"

It was as if I had slapped her in the face. She recoiled, looking at me incredulously. "You're a *what*?"

"I went to church with Andrew and Bonnie, and I gave my life to Christ. I'm a born-again Christian." The words coming out of my mouth sounded goofy to me as well. They were too out of character to be true, but there they were.

Lise knew all too well how angry I had been at God and how much I distrusted and resented most Christians. For years she had listened as I condemned televangelists as crooks and ridiculed neighbors who invited her to Bible studies.

She looked me dead in the eye. "You don't fool around with stuff like that, David." She imagined the heavens opening up and lightning bolts being cast down upon us. She was actually afraid. Lise had grown up in a French Catholic home, so the concepts of a personal relationship with God and being "born again" were completely foreign. She saw God as an all-powerful, stern disciplinarian shaking his finger at her, not someone you could have a relationship with. And yet, it was obvious that what had happened to me was real. Lise didn't understand it, but something about me had changed.

My conversion prompted her own spiritual journey, which ended with her wrestling with Christ and then surrendering her life to him two weeks later. I watched God turn her life upside down as she cried a river of tears. I was discovering that encountering Jesus does that to you.

Donavon, who was 11 at the time, and Jasmine, age 9, followed suit a few days later. Always independent-minded, Jasmine insisted on doing things her own way. As Donavon knelt and prayed, Jasmine announced, "I know Jesus loves me, but I'm not going to say my prayer today. I'm going to wait until my birthday next week, and I'm going to say my prayer under a tree in the park. That way I'll always remember it."

"Let the little children come to me, and do not hinder them, for the kingdom of heaven belongs to such as these" (Matthew 19:14, *New International Version*).

Chapter 17
I Can See Clearly Now

"Whenever, though, they turn to face God as Moses
did, God removes the veil and there they are — face-
to-face! They suddenly recognize that God is a living,
personal presence, not a piece of chiseled stone. [. . .]
And so we are transfigured much like the Messiah, our
lives gradually becoming brighter and more beautiful
as God enters our lives and we become like him."
—2 Corinthians 3:16–18, *The Message*

In the days after my final surrender, I felt like something had
broken inside of me. All of my resistance was gone. I also
found I was much more sensitive to those around me. My
indifference to the strangers I interacted with daily shifted
to a warm curiosity. Suddenly, I saw Starbucks baristas as
people, not merely purveyors of coffee. It felt as if someone
had turned up the intensity of life. Profanity, which I had used
frequently, now stung my ears, and I could see, hear, and feel
what was going on around me better than ever before.

When I reflected on my transformation during quieter
moments, I still had doubts. Was I merely grasping at straws
in a weak moment? This line of thinking led me back to
the place where it all started: church. I knew I had felt an

awesome presence, a force of some kind. This mysterious energy had washed over me in huge, unrelenting waves not once but three Sundays in a row, making me cry like I'd never cried before. I also reflected on the day I invited God into my life, how I had felt his love and acceptance, and how a lifetime of sin had flashed before me in an instant. It was as if a veil had been lifted. For the first time, I saw how lost, empty, and pointless my life had been. I felt my old self dying and slipping away, and it hurt.

I invited Brent Cantelon, the head pastor of Bonnie's church, to my home and shared my concerns. Brent was a slim, energetic man about my age. He came from a long line of pastors in the Pentecostal tradition and spoke with a quiet confidence that made him easy to understand and believe. He patiently explained what he thought had happened that day. "What you felt those first three Sundays was the presence of the Holy Spirit," he said. "As a Pentecostal church, we believe in and pursue the presence and gifts of the Holy Spirit. The Holy Spirit is God, and God is pure and perfect love. So when you prayed and asked God to fill you with his Spirit that day, he did."

I shifted uneasily in my recliner and struggled to put words to my next question. Brent was such a nice man and was clearly very knowledgeable, so I didn't want to offend him or insult his intelligence, but I needed an answer. "Brent, I made this decision based on feelings and an experience I had at church. I took this leap of faith with my heart, not my mind. I know next to nothing about the Bible and whether or not it's true. I'm used to making decisions based on data, not feelings."

Brent listened patiently as I expressed my concerns (pastors need a lot of patience). After I finished unloading, he explained that God speaks to us in a number of ways: through his Word, the Bible; through prayer; through the Holy Spirit;

and through fellowship with other believers. Then Brent encouraged me to relax and settle in for the ride. "There will be peaks and there will be valleys, but God never gives you more than you can handle."

I also shared the difficulty I had understanding the Old Testament, except for Proverbs, which I really enjoyed as wisdom literature. Brent understood and encouraged me to stick with the New Testament for the first while. "Get to know the person of Jesus first." Brent also suggested that I start my days quietly. "Take time to pray and read your Bible first thing in the morning."

So that's what I did. I started each day in my home office — my man cave — which is an 800-square-foot building situated at the rear of our 1-acre property. Butting up against a small forest of evergreen trees, it's the envy of all my buddies, with a full rack of dumbbells, a chin-up bar, an exercise bike, and a nice living room area with a flat-screen TV. Oh yeah, it also has an office area.

Taking Brent's advice, I started in the New Testament and found that Christ's words jumped off the page. His boldness was breathtaking. Jesus had no home, money, earthly possessions, status, or position of authority. He stood up for the little guys and told you to love your enemies, feed the hungry, clothe the naked, take in strangers, and care for widows and orphans. He hung out with prostitutes and criminals. He had no time for pompous religious types who used religion to control and oppress people, and he told them so. He also made it perfectly clear that the first would be last, that the last would be first, and that the meek would inherit the earth. With a message like that, it's no wonder that the early church was filled with the poor, the sick, and the downtrodden.

I also felt an immediate connection with Matthew, the Jewish tax collector; we were both in controversial businesses. Jesus walked by his booth one day, turned to Matthew, and simply said, "Follow me." No discussion, no debate. Matthew got up and walked away from his profitable business forever. He was a man of action — my kind of guy.

Chapter 18
From Profit to Purpose

"Blessed are the poor in spirit,
for theirs is the kingdom of heaven."
—Matthew 5:3, *NIV*

Back at work in my large corner office, I surveyed the wall, which was filled with graphs and charts. These were the critical numbers by which I ran my company. Branch by branch, business by business, we tracked our loan volumes. They were going up, way up, and for the first time ever, I couldn't have cared less. The more I struggled to make sense of my new faith and the business I was in, the more I realized the two didn't fit. The only thing at work that I did care about was the benevolent fund we had started a year earlier after meeting Ellen, a.k.a. Street Mom.

Taking a page out of Mike's book, I had established a structured giving plan.

The company had a monthly budget of $10,000 that we gave to organizations that provided food, shelter, or support services to the homeless and mentally ill. Responsibility for this budget rotated from department to department and city to city. Each group established a committee of volunteer employees who went into their community to identify potential recipients. Every month, we blessed an assortment of homeless shelters, housing societies, and mental-health support groups. We also established a fund that matched all money employees raised or donated to these same causes. As a result, the spirit of giving took on a life of its own within the organization.

A variety of fundraising efforts, such as raffles and bake sales, sprang up.

Employees started a Secret Santa Society, which I happily matched dollar for dollar.

The society would identify a family in need, buy groceries and gifts, and then drop the packages off on their doorstep, ring the bell, and run away. Participants came back beaming with pride and joy at being part of something so meaningful.

They got so much out of it that they decided Santa should visit year-round. If others missed the irony of us playing Santa Claus to the poor, I certainly didn't. But I didn't care; it felt right.

Meanwhile, God was birthing some other ideas in me.

* * * * *

The loud buzzer gave me access to the shelter through a heavy metal door. As I stepped inside, the antiseptic odors stung my nostrils. Lonely, empty faces stared up as I passed. I took a deep breath. *I can do this.*

Triage is the name of an emergency shelter operated by the Rain City Housing and Support Society on Vancouver's Downtown East Side. This area is widely known as Canada's poorest postal code, and it's infamous for its open-air drug market. The neighborhood explodes into what locals call "Mardi Gras" once a month on welfare Wednesdays. For many people, it is the last stop on the way out of mainstream society, and most never return.

The saddest players in this tragic comedy are the mentally ill. They end up at the shelter as a result of an indifferent government's failed attempts to support them in the community instead of in institutions. Alone on the streets, these most vulnerable citizens are easy prey for hustlers, pimps, and drug dealers.

As the surprise recipients of one of our $10,000 donations, the people at Triage felt compelled to invite us down for a tour. Leslie, the shelter manager, was our guide. She was a passionate, articulate lady in her 30s with a curious blend of intelligence and street smarts, which she came by honestly. She knew these streets from the other side of the counter as well.

As we walked, she told me about their transitional housing strategy and how the shelter was the starting point, a short-stay facility designed to stabilize the tenants and prepare them for independent living elsewhere. Half listening, I nodded, feeling oddly voyeuristic as I peered into the empty cinder-block rooms. The walls were painted drab yellow. Metal bed-frames were bolted to the wall and covered with thin, plastic-coated mattresses. I couldn't help but think of how many places like this my mother had called home.

When the tour was over, we adjourned to Leslie's office for a cup of coffee. As we relaxed, I told her about my mother. She listened with the empathy of someone who trades in such experiences daily.

Near the end of our time together, I asked Leslie what she saw as their greatest need. Her eyes lit up immediately. "Women. There is a *big* crack in the system that women are falling through." She explained that the city's hardest-to-house ladies were getting kicked out of shelters and rooming houses because their behavior was so aggressive and erratic. These ladies usually had a clinically diagnosed mental illness, were addicted to drugs, and were also active in the sex trade.

They became trapped on a merry-go-round of shelters, jails, and psychiatric wards. As Leslie explained that a minimum-barrier, women-only housing option was what these ladies needed, a light went on inside of me.

Chapter 19
The Vivian

The derelict, 24-room rooming house was vacant except for one elderly Chinese gentleman. He was deaf and had been a tenant in the same 100-square-foot room for over 25 years, during which he had worked as a dishwasher in a Chinatown restaurant. As I poked my head into the room and looked at the frightened little man with two huge hearing aids, it was like entering another world.

The building was located on the "lower stroll," a place where the lowest-priced prostitutes plied their trade. The women there were so sick, broken, and desperate that it was hard to imagine what possible sexual attraction their tricks had. The depravity of man knows no bounds.

The owner of the building, Mr. Chow, spoke no English. Somehow, through his job as a cook on the ferries that ran back and forth between Vancouver and various islands off the coast, he had saved enough money to acquire several rooming houses in the area, all of which he owned free and clear. Mr. Chow looked like a poor pensioner, but he was actually a multimillionaire.

Through my interpreter, I learned that Mr. Chow and his wife had raised their family in the owner's suite on the main floor of the building while renting out the 24 rooms on the second and third floors. Tenants shared bathrooms and showers down the hall. Like many buildings in the area, this rooming house had been built in the early 1900s as short-term accommodations for single men who worked on ships or in the lumber and mining camps. As the resource sectors declined, the tenant demographics shifted. The elderly Chows weren't equipped to manage the mentally ill, drug-addicted, and criminally active tenants flooding the area. What was once their family home was now a near-vacant skid row rooming house. It met our needs perfectly.

After brief negotiations, I bought the property, hired contractors, and began renovations. Lise and I felt that it was important for all of us to play a physical part in the process, so we worked as a family with friends and volunteers. The ladies and kids painted and cleaned while 12-year-old Donavon and I tore stuff down in the backyard and filled a container with a ton of debris. Frugal as he was, Mr. Chow hadn't wanted to spend money on dump fees. Instead, he had used his backyard as a landfill, concealing waste lumber and building materials under several layers of dirt. It was totally illegal, but an offence of that degree didn't raise an eyebrow on the Downtown East Side, where not even parking meters were monitored. We poured our hearts into the work. Like my mother, the ladies who would call the rooming house home had been abused for much of their lives. We wanted them to feel safe and secure.

When opening day arrived, Leslie asked if I would mind naming the building after my mother. I was both touched and honored. The Vivian, or the Viv, became home to 24 of Vancouver's hardest of hard-to-house women.

*   *   *   *   *

Today, Rain City Housing manages and staffs the Vivian with social workers 24 hours a day, seven days a week. Rain City isn't a faith-based organization, so they have no spiritual agenda or standards that residents have to meet. These ladies, many of whom are still addicts and active in the sex trade, are taken as they are and where they are, with a view toward wellness that will help them transition one day to healthy, independent living.

The Vivian represents a highly controversial, groundbreaking approach to homelessness. It was the first dual-diagnosis program of its kind. Before it opened, addiction and mental health issues were treated separately. Now they are being treated as interrelated conditions.

Because the ladies who call the Viv home arrive fully active in the lifestyles that put them there, critics contend the program enables prostitution and drug addiction. Supporters counter that this minimum-barrier housing model is a necessary first step toward breaking the cycle of homelessness. I believe that both are true. A warm and safe place to sleep, a regular healthy diet, consistent use of their prescribed psychiatric medications, and ready access to in-house visits from a psychiatrist all contribute to the ladies' mental and physical wellness. This newfound health gives them strength and energy that "enables" them to be even more active in the harmful things that brought them there in the first place. This is undeniable. What is equally true, however, is that some of these ladies are able to use this new strength and courage to confront their past and begin a new and better life. At the Vivian, the wins are few, but we still see them.

When Leslie came to me with the idea for this unique kind of housing, she had Patty, a schizophrenic drug addict, in mind. Patty weighed all of 100 pounds and had been a beautiful young lady before her mind and body were ravaged by mental illness and drug addiction. Patty was a regular at the emergency shelter. Leslie would get calls from friends on the street or the police saying, "Patty's lying naked in the middle of Hastings Street, and she's blasted." Leslie would rush out, throw Patty over her shoulder, and march her back to the shelter. A few days later, Patty would be back on the streets. In the ten months between January and October 2004, before the Vivian opened, Patty was hospitalized 89 times. In her first year at the Viv, she was hospitalized twice. "The money the system saved on Patty could furnish and staff the Vivian for a year," Patty's psychiatrist said.

Patty now lives in a small community far away from the craziness of the Downtown East Side. She is 33, married, and doing well. Patty's mother says there's no mystery as to her success. "The Vivian saved my daughter's life."

When the Viv opened, Patty's mom wanted to thank me for helping her daughter. "I have two daughters," she said. "They were raised the same, but Patty ended up on the Downtown East Side." Over coffee, I talked about my mum, and she talked about Patty. We both cried.

Patty's mother is a good woman who loves her daughter. She spent countless nights searching skid row trying to rescue her mentally ill child, to no avail. It felt so good to know that the Vivian brought her and Patty's anguish to an end.

* * * * *

My attempt to reconcile the pain of my mother's life and bring meaning to my newfound wealth became a turning point in my spiritual pilgrimage. This new and generous way of living stirred something deep and unexpected within me. I began experiencing a new sense of warmth, a peaceful, joyful presence that filled the profound emptiness I walked with every day of my life.

Lise and I also noticed that working at the Vivian had drawn us closer together as a family. Putting our faith into action felt right, and we wanted more.

Chapter 20
Homes of Hope

The smell of garbage in the gutters stung our nostrils as my family and I bounced in the back of an old, battered van. It was early morning, but my shirt was already sticking to the back of the cheap vinyl seat. I stared out at shacks made of scrap lumber, sheet metal, and plastic tarps. Half-starved, filthy mongrel dogs sniffed hopefully through the trash. They looked up at us with sad, vacant eyes. Clusters of little boys with short, shiny, sharply parted black hair and girls with long, bouncing ponytails, all in clean school uniforms, stood at odds with the gloomy landscape. *Unbelievable,* I thought. *How do people live like this?*

We were in the Colonias, an impoverished area in Tijuana where we were to spend the weekend helping to build a home for a poor family. Working on the Downtown East Side had been a special experience for us. We wanted to serve in other practical ways, which is what led us to Mexico. This was our first time up close and personal with this level of poverty, and it wasn't pretty.

Finally, our van stopped. We climbed out, uncertain of our surroundings but happy to be off the drunken rollercoaster ride through the dusty hills. We gathered around our leader as he introduced the Gonzales family, who was to be the recipient of our efforts.

The father, Felipe, a thin, sallow man, looked down and away. The mother, Julieta, looked up with a pleading smile and sad, darting eyes. Pablo, 20, stood next to his mother, eyes closed, slumped, his wiry frame swaying back and forth as he groaned. The odd grin on his face exposed dirty, twisted teeth. He was severely mentally handicapped and totally blind. The matriarch of this clan, Isabella, was the oldest and shortest lady I had ever seen. She stood not an inch over 4 feet in her tattered black dress. The hope and pride of the Gonzales family was Gabriela, a beautiful young lady of 16 with long, black hair. Her large, dark, penetrating eyes asked, "Why us?"

Their home, which was smaller than our smallest bedroom, was an old garage door teetering against scrap plywood and corrugated metal. The roof was a dirty plastic tarp that clearly did not keep out the rain. The dirt floors were muddy; their hovel, cold. Everything inside — clothing, blankets, and furniture — was damp.

The Gonzales family was one of thousands of peasant families streaming into Tijuana every year in search of a better life. They all shared the same dream: a job in the *maquiladoras,* one of the massive factories owned by large multinational corporations that make electronics, clothing, and car parts for their U.S. neighbors. But like so many other families, their dream of financial security turned into a nightmare. Unable to find work, they were forced onto the streets, where they panhandled and picked through trash. Finally, Felipe found a job as a security guard. He worked 12 hours a day, six days a week to feed his family. After years of hard work, they had saved the $400 down payment required to buy the tiny piece of dirt on which their shack sat from a "developer," who carried the financing. All they needed now was a house.

It was already sweltering at 9:00 a.m. We stood in stunned silence as our leader explained how in two short days we would transform the freshly poured concrete slab and huge pile of building materials that sat next to the Gonzaleses' shack into a home for their family. I wouldn't have believed the young man if he were not part of a much bigger organization called Homes of Hope, a Youth With A Mission (YWAM) ministry, one of the largest missionary organizations in the world. Homes of Hope had been down there for 15 years and built thousands of similar homes for families in Tijuana and Ensenada. I had discovered Homes of Hope through business associate and fellow EO member David Steele. The Steeles had been coming down with other EO members and friends for a few years.

Our ragtag group of 22 construction workers — men, women, and children from ages 4 to 74 — were a very unlikely crew. Clearly, we needed supernatural intervention, so before we set to work, we joined hands and bowed our heads. "Lord, you are our God. We thank you for bringing us here today and giving us an opportunity to share your love with this family. We pray for your protection as we work today and that you will bless the Gonzales family and the home we build. In Jesus' name we pray, Amen."

I opened my eyes and looked into the tear-streaked face of Mama Julieta, who had locked arms with her son. I felt a sudden lump in my throat. *It's not fair,* I thought. *How does this happen?*

* * * * *

The men and boys divided up into framing and truss crews while the ladies and the girls started to paint. After two days of SWAT team–like effort, our motley crew was standing in a circle once again. This time, though, a giddy excitement filled the air. We were sunburned and covered in paint, and our muscles were sore. I had hit my thumb with a hammer at least a dozen times. But we were happy, and our hearts were full. The house was complete, and it was beautiful.

The freshly painted, 400-square-foot home had a locking door, windows, and an asphalt shingle roof. We had also bought brand-new furniture, including beds, a table, chairs, and a gas stove, and we stocked the shelves with groceries and a few gifts for the kids. For the first time in many years, the Gonzales family would sleep in a dry, safe, and secure home.

As is tradition with Homes of Hope, our building foreman locked the door and then handed the keys to the youngest member of our team, a sweet little 4-year-old girl. Through a translator, we took turns sharing words of encouragement and blessing with the family. Crew members talked about how much building the home meant to them and how they hoped it would help the Gonzales family in the future.

Mama Juliet stood between her little mother and her son, bottom lip quivering, tears rolling down her face. "Gracias," she managed to say, and then she nodded, unable to speak any further.

Felipe remained stone-faced, but he glanced up from the ground long enough to echo his wife's sentiments. "Gracias."

After one of the dads on our team spoke a heartfelt prayer of blessing over the family and their home, the little girl stepped forward with her arm fully extended, a big smile on her face, and held out the keys for Julieta. She unlocked the door and led her family into their new home for the very first time. After giving them a few moments, all 25 of us crammed inside and joined the family on the grand tour.

It was a joyful and, for some, tearful experience watching the family try to process their incredible good fortune. I felt convicted by the disproportionate relationship between our sacrifice — a mere two days of our time — and the blessing it provided to this family. It required so little of us, but it meant so much to them.

As we loaded our tools and equipment into the vans for the bumpy ride back to the Homes of Hope base, I glanced back and saw Mama Julieta gently pressing her blind son's hand on the wall of their new home and whispering in his ear.

Mum and Dad, "Newlyweds" in happier times. *(Undated)*

Brothers Paul and Peter on the balcony with David. *(Circa 1967)*

David Ash

David and Mum hanging out. *(Circa 1989)*

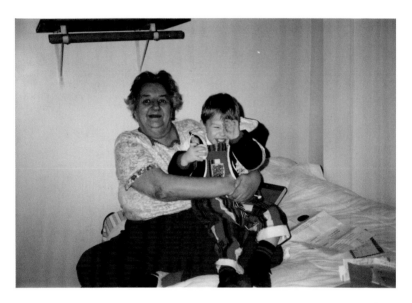

Mum and Donavon (2). Her one and only
visit with her grandson. *(Circa 1994)*

David Ash

David and Donavon (6) at Payroll Loans headquarters. *(Circa 1998)*

Jasmine (4) and Donavon (6) in front of the first
Payroll Loans retail outlet. *(Circa 1998)*

David, Lise and Jasmine with Dad's new
Porsche Boxster. *(Circa 1998)*

Donavon and Jasmine with Ellen Shonsta,
AKA Street Mom. *(Circa 2002)*

For Donavon's 10th birthday, instead of presents he asked
for donations to Street Mom's ministry. *(Circa 2002)*

Family vacation. *(Circa 2004)*

David Ash

Front exterior of the Vivian. *(May, 2016)*

David and Nigel in the backyard of the Vivian. *(May, 2016)*

Mike sharing his story at Be Brave Ranch. *(May, 2016)*

Glori, Lise, Mike, Jane and David reunite
at Be Brave Ranch. *(May, 2016)*

David Ash

David, Glori and Mike tour the main building
at Be Brave Ranch. *(May, 2016)*

Lise, Jane, Glori, Mike and David jamming in the
music room at Be Brave Ranch. *(May, 2016)*

Chapter 21
From Costa Rica to Kona

On our last night in Tijuana, Lise and I had the pleasure of meeting Sean Lambert, the founder of Homes of Hope. Sean could easily be mistaken for a successful American business-man. He was a tall, heavyset, silver-haired man in his 40s with a friendly demeanor and a "let's get it done" kind of energy that one feels around entrepreneurial types. His wife Janet was an attractive, passionate lady with sandy blond hair. Together with their three beautiful daughters, who were in their late teens, they had been volunteer missionaries in YWAM for over 20 years.

"Volunteers?" I asked, struggling to mask my disbelief.

Sean explained that YWAM was a volunteer-only orga-nization. Everyone from the top to the bottom had to raise their own support from friends, relatives, and their church. "It hasn't been an easy life," he said, "but it has been a great life. We wouldn't trade it for anything. God has always been faithful."

Sean went on to describe how they had been able to raise their daughters in San Diego and still travel all over the world as a family serving God. They believed these trips were invalu-able educational opportunities for their girls, all of whom were also able to attend university. "We have a supporter who committed to pay for the girls' education if they wanted it."

That night we learned that Homes of Hope was only one of hundreds of YWAM bases around the world. YWAM also operates medical clinics; orphanages; a Mercy Ships ministry, which brings aid to remote islands; and ministries to women, children at risk, prisons, and more — almost any kind of humanitarian work or ministry you can imagine.

I was also surprised to learn that YWAM has its own university, the University of the Nations (U of N). With a unique decentralized, modular structure, they have educational programs in biblical studies, evangelism, writing, filmmaking, photography, alternative energy, water systems, and medical relief.

Sean explained that like the U of N, YWAM as a whole is completely decentralized. Every base operates independently. There is no central authority that provides funding or exercises executive control. Instead, the bases are held together by a shared vision, mission, and purpose. The width and breadth of this global organization was staggering, especially when I considered that all of the full- and part-time staff were volunteers. As a business owner, I knew how hard it was to keep everyone on task when they were being paid good salaries. I couldn't imagine what it was like to have to manage and motivate volunteers.

At the end of the evening, Sean mentioned that he would be in Vancouver soon. We invited him to drop by if he had time.

* * * * *

Not long after we returned from Mexico, Sean called to say he was in town. As it turned out, the only time we could meet was the night of our weekly Bible study, which was at our house.

David Ash

Disappointed that we couldn't spend more time together, we agreed to meet for an early dinner before our friends arrived.

Around this time, Lise and I had been exploring ways we could become more active and grow in our faith. We didn't feel that two hours at church on Sunday and a Bible study was allowing us to grow fast enough spiritually. Our trip to Tijuana had been part of our effort to get more involved. Like most people, we had busy lives. I was running my company, and Lise was homeschooling the kids. However, I was also in the process of stepping back from day-to-day operations, and I suggested we might take a three-month break, a sabbatical, at the end of the year. It would be a perfect opportunity to grow in our faith. I had visions of sipping an early-morning coffee on the balcony of a beautiful beachfront condominium in Costa Rica as I read my Bible.

As we sat in the backyard with Sean that evening, I told him about my Costa Rican plan, asking if he could connect us with a YWAM base there. Perhaps we could help build another house or volunteer at an orphanage. Sean listened patiently until we were finished. Then he gave us his gentle response. "I think the Costa Rican thing would be fun for you, David, but Lise will still be busy homeschooling the kids. And honestly, I don't know that three months in Costa Rica is going to help either of you grow spiritually."

Wow, I thought, *Sean is a straight shooter.* I was a little taken aback, but it was also incredibly refreshing. One of my greatest frustrations in recent years had been people's tendency to agree — or at least not disagree — with me. I'd grown to love people who challenged my thinking. "What do you suggest?" I asked.

Just then, the phone rang. Lise picked it up. It was one of the couples from our Bible study group saying they couldn't make it. It was a good reminder we were running out of time, and we were both anxious to hear whatever Sean had to say.

We resumed our discussion, but five minutes later, the phone rang again.

Another couple canceled. We were down to one couple. The phone rang again. Lise and I looked at each other. *Could it be?*

"Something came up," she said after she hung up. "They can't make it, either."

Three couples, three last-minute cancelations. Home group was canceled. It had never happened before, and it hasn't happened since. We had Sean to ourselves for the entire evening.

As I fired up the barbeque, Sean went on to describe a five-month program YWAM offered called Discipleship Training School (DTS). He thought it would be perfect for us. It would involve our living as a family on a YWAM base in Kona, Hawaii, for a three-month lecture phase, followed by a two-month outreach somewhere in the world. Best of all, there was a school on the base where the kids could study while we were in class. We would also eat in an open-air cafeteria with hundreds of other volunteer staff and students, so Lise wouldn't have to worry about meals. The more Sean spoke, the more Lise's eyes lit up. No homeschooling for five months *and* no cooking? In a matter of minutes, I saw my Costa Rican dream vanish before my eyes.

Chapter 22
The University of the Nations

The months after Sean's visit flew by. Lise had a hundred and one family things to think about, and I had my business. There was a lot to do.

The moment of truth arrived two weeks before we left for our YWAM Discipleship Training School in Hawaii. As I sat in the large boardroom of my lawyer's 35th-floor office and surveyed the piles of file folders in front of me, my chest tightened. This was by far the largest financial transaction of my career, and it represented the culmination of my life's work. The company was larger and more profitable than ever. We had recently invested over $3 million in new technology that would allow the business to grow faster than ever before. Our best years were ahead of us.

My tough, no-nonsense corporate lawyer gave me a cynical "Are you *sure* you want to do this?" look and then opened a file folder. As he explained the structure of the complex transaction, I scanned the document and realized that my signature at the bottom of these pages would trigger the irrevocable sale of the most profitable company I had ever owned, and likely would ever own, in my life. I'd be leaving the power, authority, and status behind forever.

The sale was structured as an MBO (management buyout), which meant my management team would pay the sale price out of profits over the next five years. It was a huge risk if the managers made a mistake or were dishonest. Luckily, I had total confidence in my team. I trusted them like family, because they were: My brothers Peter and Paul, who had joined me early on as employees, had been a huge part of the company's success. They were happy to take over, and I was happy to hand them the reins. Grabbing the pen, I took a deep breath and a huge leap into the hands of God.

* * * * *

The entire family was crammed into what looked like an old motel room with a loft barely large enough to accommodate the two single mattresses on which Donavon and Jasmine slept. They loved climbing the ladder into their little "tree fort." The loft's ceiling was sloped with a 5-foot clearance at its highest point, which meant that at 6 feet, 2 inches, I had to crawl into the room when I tucked them in at night. They thought this was hilarious.

The place hadn't been renovated in 25 years, and it showed. As I went to put something away on the night of our arrival, the closet door came off in my hand. It was hot and humid, and I was tired from a long day of travel and unpacking. Frustrated, I sighed, composed myself, and leaned the door against the kitchen counter. Then I marched down the hall to our resident manager's unit and knocked on the door. Someone needed to fix this, and quick!

Bob, who also served as a biblical studies teacher and had been a missionary for 25 years, sauntered up to the screen door, smiled, and asked how I was doing. I explained my dilemma. Bob casually opened a kitchen drawer, pulled out a multi-bit screwdriver, and handed it to me with a grin. It was not the response I was expecting, but I got the message. This was not the Fairmont.

We were on YWAM's University of the Nations campus in Kona, Hawaii. It was December 28, 2004, the first night of the three-month lecture phase of our DTS. It would be followed by a two-month outreach somewhere in the world, where we would get a chance to practice what we had learned. I had thought most of my learning in the lecture phase would take place in the classroom, but that closet door was my first lesson.

* * * * *

Our days were full. We ate breakfast every morning with several hundred other students and missionaries in an open-air cafeteria. Everyone wore shorts and sandals. Small, brightly coloured birds fluttered around, chirping as they wrestled and pecked for the scraps we left behind. I learned quickly that my favourite, eggs Benny — medium poached — wasn't on the menu. But the warm Hawaiian sun and the ocean, visible from campus, made our simple breakfast of cold cereal and hard-boiled eggs taste better.

After breakfast every morning, we met in an outdoor area, called Ohana Court, for a time of passionate prayer and worship. This was followed by our classes, which ended by mid-afternoon in time for two hours of work duty. My work duty included cleaning the daycare, sweeping walkways, raking leaves, and picking up garbage — things we had land-scapers and housekeepers do for us at home.

One afternoon I was on my knees scrubbing a dirty toilet bowl in the daycare center when I chuckled to myself. *If my buddies could see me now, they'd think I'd lost my mind.* Back home, we had people who helped us manage every detail of our business and personal lives. Always traveling first-class and receiving special treatment, I had lost touch with the realities of everyday life, and it didn't feel right. I relished the opportunity to serve in practical ways and enjoyed the simplicity and obscurity of campus life.

The ground is level at the foot of the cross, and that's exactly where I wanted to be.

Chapter 23
The Priesthood of All Believers

The Discipleship Training School is where it all begins in YWAM. "To know God and to make him known" is the mission's stated purpose, and "hearing the voice of God" was the theme of our first week's teaching. I didn't fully understand this concept, but I found it fitting that Bonnie's obedience to this voice was what brought us there in the first place.

Our DTS was led by YWAM founders Loren and Darlene Cunningham. Loren, a large man in his early 70s, had the passion and energy of someone half his age and size. He was also one of the very few people in the world who had visited every sovereign nation on earth, several of them many times. He was a handsome man with Hollywood good looks, a golden tan, silver hair, and a large, white, inviting smile. Clearly brilliant, he taught with the authority of someone who had given his entire life over to his calling.

Darlene was a beautiful, energetic woman bursting with a positive energy and motherly love that affected everyone she met. Together, they were spiritual parents to thousands of YWAM missionaries around the world.

* * * * *

In class, we were taught that God could speak to us in any one of a number of ways, including the Bible, visions, dreams, a subtle inner voice, or even an audible voice. We were taught that God speaks to us all the time but that hearing his voice and discerning his message requires a sensitivity of the spirit that can only be achieved through the spiritual disciplines of forgiveness, repentance, surrender, and prayer.

One of our teachers demonstrated this principle by holding up an AM/FM radio. He turned it on, cranked up the volume, and held it in front of his microphone. Loud rock music blared through Ohana Court. He got some chuckles and shouts of "Yahoo!" from the audience.

"When we are spiritually healthy," he said, "we are able to receive communications from God. But if something happens . . ." With that, he sent the radio crashing to the floor. The room went silent. "If pride, resentment, or unforgiveness sneaks in and takes hold of your heart, your ability to hear what God is saying and feel his love will be affected."

Then he picked up the damaged radio, the dial smashed and the antenna bent at a right angle, and explained that God wants to use us as a conduit for his love to the world around us. "But if your radio is broken, you're not going to hear or feel his presence in your life."

All students were encouraged to start their days with a quiet time, reading their Bible, meditating, and writing in their journals. So every morning I got up an hour or two ahead of everyone, made a mug full of hot coffee, and snuck out to the sanctuary of our van. As odd as it sounds, it was there that I began to feel the presence of God in a new way. The words of the Bible seemed to jump off the page. Having been such a close friend of sin, I knew truth when I saw it, and it cut to my heart like a double-edged sword. After one or two hours alone, reading, praying, and journaling, I didn't want to leave. When I did, I would float out of the van with a new inner strength, ready to take on the day.

*　*　*　*　*

I thanked my classmate as he handed me the book *There Is Always Enough*. It was the story of Heidi and Rolland Baker's ministry in Africa. John was excited as he described some of the supernatural things happening there. Lise and I were taking a weekend break off base with the kids, so I promised I'd give it a scan over the weekend.

Lise and the kids were anxious to hit the beach in Waikiki, so I encouraged them to go on ahead while I had a little quiet time. I promised to catch up shortly. As I sat alone reading in the hotel room, I found myself drawn in by the Bakers' experiences in Mozambique.

It was 1995, and the civil war had just ended. Roads, villages, bridges, schools, and hospitals had been blown up. The country's infrastructure was all but wiped out. Savage torture and killing had taken place. Years of drought had added famine to the war. Thousands of men, women, and children wandered around in dark, burnt-out villages without food, clothing, or medical care. There was only one doctor for every 40,000 people in the country. It was then, at the lowest point in Mozambique's history, that the Bakers decided to start an orphanage that took in the worst of the worst children. These boys and girls had been living on the streets, roaming, scavenging, stealing, fighting, and begging for food. Against the advice of local churches and authorities, who encouraged them to help other good Christian families and forget these "bad kids," the Bakers went after society's castaways, "the very least of these."

The more I read, the more captivated I became. I found the book impossible to put down. The life of total abandonment and passion that these people lived, striving to be the literal hands and feet of Jesus, was infectious. My heart cried out to serve God with all that I had, but I felt totally inadequate. I didn't know where to start. How could I ever match the example set by these people?

When I finally took a break from reading, I did what we were trained to do when we needed direction: I prayed. "God," I said, "I am yours. I want to serve you with all of my heart. Please guide me, lead me, and show me what you want me to do."

With that, I opened my Bible to a random spot and read the two chapters in front of me, Ephesians 3–4. As I read, I found myself particularly moved by Ephesians 4:1–6:

> As a prisoner for the Lord, then, I urge you to live a life worthy of the calling you have received. Be completely humble and gentle; be patient, bearing with one another in love. Make every effort to keep the unity of the Spirit through the bond of peace. There is one body and one Spirit, just as you were called to one hope when you were called; one Lord, one faith, one baptism; one God and Father of all, who is over all and through all and in all.

Being the good DTS student that I was, I took a few moments to journal my thoughts on this scripture. When I was finished, I picked up *There Is Always Enough* and continued where I had left off.

At that point in the story, Heidi was talking about taking a break and visiting the Toronto Airport Church. She explained that their work in Mozambique with orphans had been fruitful but that the rest of their ministry had hit a wall. They had planted only four churches in their entire time there. She was exhausted and burnt out:

> I was utterly and completely helpless. I've never been so humbled, never felt so poor, so helpless, so vulnerable. I was a type-A, driven person, and God had to break and humble me. He showed me my total inadequacy to do anything in my own strength. The Lord spoke to me about relinquishing control to Him. He showed me that I needed to learn to work with the rest of the Body of Christ.

God then led Heidi to a scripture that marked the turning point in their lives and ministry. When they returned to Mozambique, their work exploded, from four struggling churches to over 5,000 in Mozambique and 10,000 globally, not to mention well-drilling programs, free health clinics, feeding programs, primary and secondary schools, Bible schools, and other community outreach programs.

What was that ministry-transforming scripture? The hair on the back of my neck stood up as I read it over and over again; Ephesians 4:1–6, the very passage I had turned to at random and journaled about only moments earlier!

My New Testament Bible had 510 pages with 23,145 verses. The odds of my randomly turning to and being inspired by the same scripture that transformed the Bakers' ministry, only minutes before I read it in their book, were beyond calculation. In that moment, my doubts vanished. God had reached across the great divide and said, "David, I am here."

* * * * *

The day had started with our teachers regaling us with tales of missionary adventures in developing countries that they had experienced 30 years earlier. We heard stories of miraculous last-minute provisions of food and funds occurring after acts of obedience, faith, and generosity to the poor. Our leaders taught us that the first disciples lived in community and shared everything: "All the believers were together and had everything in common. They sold property and possessions to give to anyone who had need" (Acts 2:44–45, *NIV*).

At the end of the day, they encouraged us to participate in an exercise that modeled this selfless lifestyle. They suggested we ask God if there was anyone in the room with whom we should share our resources.

After praying, I watched as my classmates milled about excitedly. Students went up to people they didn't know and gave away their guitar, their favorite jacket, or money. Crying, laughing, and praying were happening all around us. It was a beautiful sight to behold, but I felt left out.

The focus of the day's teaching was living by faith and trusting God to provide for all of our needs as we served him. This was held up as an incredibly adventurous and fulfilling way to live. As I listened to this, I couldn't help but wonder where that left me. I could have met every financial need in the room, and I wouldn't have even noticed the money was gone. Was I supposed give everything away to follow God? Did I even belong here — not just in that room but in God's kingdom?

The next morning we had a surprise visitor, a successful entrepreneur named David who had developed a chain of fitness facilities in the U.S. After a brief introduction, Loren invited David to share his experience as a Christian in the marketplace.

This handsome, well-dressed middle-aged businessman *looked* like someone who owned a chain of fitness centers. As he took the mike, it was clear he was more at home in his gyms than in front of us. After saying a few kind words about

YWAM, his voice began to crack, but he continued. "Most people don't understand how Christian business guys feel," he said. "We want to be a part of the work of God like anyone else." To our surprise, he began to break down. "Some people make us feel like making money is dirty or a less-than-holy pursuit. Sometimes it feels like all anyone wants from us is our checkbook. It's like we're on the outside looking in. If you guys want to minister to businesspeople, you need to treat them like everyone else."

A hush fell over the room. We were caught off-guard by our visitor's spontaneous transparency. As he continued, he became less and less coherent and increasingly emotional.

While I sat in the audience watching this poor man have a meltdown, I was having one of my own. His pain was my pain. He was articulating the cries of my heart perfectly. I was moved by a sudden, overwhelming compulsion to jump into the ring with this guy, to support him, to say something. Exactly what, I wasn't sure.

Unable to restrain myself, I marched up to the front and asked if I could say a few words. As I took the microphone with my nose running and tears streaming down my face, I plunged forward, ignoring my inhibitions. "I can totally relate to everything David is saying," I said. "I am a business-man back home, and I often feel like all anyone wants from me is my money. During yesterday's exercise I felt excluded, but today I see things differently." Like David's, my message became less coherent as I got more emotional. What did come through clearly though was my pain and the sense of isolation I felt.

When Loren took the microphone back, he did what he always did: He directed us back to the Word. "I'm not overly impressed by the fact that someone is rich," Loren said. "I am best friends with the richest guy in the world. He owns the cattle on a thousand hills. He owns the world and everything in it."

This got a chuckle, and the emotional energy in the room shifted as he continued. "The separation between the sacred and the secular is a manmade division that has nothing to do with God or his plan for your life. The Bible is very clear about this in First Peter, Chapter 2. 'But you are a chosen people, a royal priesthood, a holy nation, God's special possession, that you may declare the praises of him who called you out of darkness into his wonderful light.' As a follower of Jesus, whether you're a housewife, a student, a garage mechanic, or an entrepreneur, you are automatically a member of the priesthood of all believers. After your DTS, most of you will go home to families and careers. When you do, each of you has your own unique ministry. Your calling is as important as any full-time pastor's or missionary's; there is no hierarchy in Christ."

Up until then, Lise and I had been doing our DTS in stealth mode. When meeting new people, I would admit to being a businessman back home, but nobody had an inkling of the degree of my success. Finally, in a small way, I had outed myself to my classmates. I no longer felt like I had to hide or be ashamed. Thanks to a random visitor, I had heard exactly what I needed to hear exactly when I needed to hear it. A pattern was emerging.

Chapter 24
Outreach

It was dark as I climbed the stairs to the roof of the building in Medan, Indonesia. The night was silent except for crickets chirping and a dog barking two doors down. I looked out over the large, dusty city full of strangers. Random lights silhouetted concrete structures connected by the tangled wires that brought them power.

Alone, I searched for a stable plastic chair to sit on and another one for my books. It was 80 degrees Fahrenheit at 4:30 a.m., but the rooftop was a relief from the airless little room I had just left. Getting a good night's sleep was almost impossible. Environmental controls in Indonesia were virtually nonexistent. During the day, the 96-degree heat and 98 percent relative humidity was draining. I was tired all the time. Worn down by the conditions, I found myself losing patience.

After half an hour of praying and meditating, I saw the sun peek over the horizon as a neighbor's rooster announced the start of a new day. I savored the solitude of the early morning hours and sighed in gratitude at the breeze that cooled the sweat on my forehead. I was feeling peaceful for the first time in a while when the calm was shattered by a man's voice blaring in Arabic over a loudspeaker. "Hayya 'ala-s-Salah!"

Soon, I discovered that these were rallying cries, prerecorded versions of the *adhan,* or call to prayer, coming from the mosques that surrounded the orphanage where we were volunteering. As the second of the five pillars of Islam, the prayers are played five times a day without fail in Arabic, a language that only 10 percent of Muslims speak.

I was annoyed at the interruption, and negative, angry, prideful thoughts crept into my mind. I started second-guessing our leadership, judging my teammates, and doubting the value of our contribution at the orphanage. While these thoughts played over and over in my head, I thought back to what Sean Lambert had told us before we left: "To have a good DTS, you have to surrender your rights — your right to go where you want to go and sleep where you want to sleep. At home, you are in charge. During your DTS, you are a disciple, a follower, not a leader." As I meditated on those words, alone on the roof that morning, I finally understood what C.S. Lewis meant when he said, "Pride is the complete anti-God state of mind. It is impossible to look up when you are looking down on the world around you."

Humbled and convicted, I asked God to forgive me for my pride, to empty me of myself and to fill me with his love for my teammates and the people of Indonesia. I surrendered my life to Christ — again. In that moment, my anxiousness was replaced by a peace beyond all understanding, and I received the strength to continue for another day.

A minute later, another loudspeaker a block away in the opposite direction blasted another call to prayer. Then a third and a fourth voice joined the cacophony. My quiet time was over.

* * * * *

We started each day on outreach with a team meeting on the roof after breakfast. Anna, our leader, was an attractive 26-year-old with long, straight brown hair and big brown eyes. She wore cotton dresses, sandals, headscarves, and bangles on her wrists. She would have been totally at home in an old VW van with flowers and peace signs painted on the sides. Ricardo, a 30-year-old Japanese Brazilian, played guitar while we sang and prayed together. There were 15 of us in total, most in their early 20s. Ricardo and I were two of only four guys on the team. Outnumbered, I learned to listen.

Anna gave us our assignments for the day. The guys were to paint bunk beds and do general repairs and maintenance while the girls were to teach English at the school, wash clothes, and clean up. For all of us, the highlight of each day was playing with the kids.

It became clear rather quickly that the pastor and his wife ran the institution while the kids pretty much took care of themselves, the older children forced to be the reluctant overseers of the young.

We also learned that the definition of *orphan* in Indonesia is different from back home. Only a small percentage of the children at the institution were technically orphans. Many others came from single-parent families who lived in one of the thousands of poverty-stricken villages that dotted the countryside.

The boys and girls slept in separate dormitories on homemade bunk beds that were never made. Dirty clothes were scattered everywhere; the children's hygiene was poor. Lise soon discovered that many of them had lice and initiated a delousing program immediately. Starved for attention, the children flocked to Lise's tender, nurturing care. In no time, she became the home's de facto nurse, dealing with a steady stream of real and imagined medical issues.

Lise also helped care for the only infant in the home. The baby had been orphaned in December by the tsunami that struck Banda Aceh, Indonesia, only 600 kilometers away.

Tenui, a scrappy little fellow with a mischievous glint in his eye, stole my heart right away. Whenever I saw him coming, I'd yell, "Hey, Tenui. Give me five, man!" His eyes would light up, and a big white smile would cross his little brown face as he wound up and slapped my large hand as hard as he could.

"Give me five!" he'd reply.

After wrestling with him for a bit, I would try unsuccessfully to send him on his way several times before we finally called a truce.

Meanwhile, Donavon had a blast playing soccer in the field with the tough barefoot boys, while Jasmine shadowed the girls, helping in any way she could.

* * * * *

As challenging as our time at the orphanage was, it was difficult to leave. It had become our home. After loading up our bus in the darkness of the early morning hours, we said our goodbyes to the pastor, his wife, and the kids we had grown to love.

I looked for my little buddy Tenui. When I finally found him, I held out my hand. "Give me five, man." He looked up at me, unsmiling, his arms folded tightly across his chest. He wasn't playing my game anymore.

I tried again. "Hey, Tenui. Give me five, man."

He just looked away.

Finally, I gave him a hug that wasn't returned and got on the bus. I was busted. He knew he was being left behind, abandoned once again by people he loved. As I settled into my seat, furious tears flooded my eyes. I couldn't reconcile the injustice of it all.

David Ash

Chapter 25
Surrendering — Again

"No one can serve two masters. Either you will hate the one
and love the other, or you will be devoted to the one and
despise the other. You cannot serve both God and money."
—Matthew 6:24, *NIV*

After outreach, our team returned to Kona for a one-week
debriefing. Prior to our DTS, I had cynically assumed that
YWAM's ranks were filled with idealistic dropouts who
couldn't make it in the real world. Nothing could be further
from the truth. Over the last five months, we had met people
from all walks of life who had left promising careers and large
incomes to be the hands and feet of Jesus. These men and
women who had rejected the world's success-obsessed value
system in favor of God's had opened our eyes to a whole new
way of living that was filled with meaning and adventure. We
also knew that our busy lives were waiting for us at home,
and we didn't want our newfound passion to be muted by our
hectic, affluent schedules. Only an authentic, vibrant faith
would sustain us, and we were prepared to do whatever was
necessary to keep that alive.

* * * * *

I stared at the documents in front of me. The spreadsheet summarized every single asset we owned — real estate, stocks, bonds, mortgages, and cash. It represented the culmination of my life's work, everything for which I had risked, fought, and sacrificed. I felt a fear as I never had before.

I had believed the motivational speakers 25 years earlier. They were right: Persistence and determination are powerful. No matter who you are or where you're from, with a positive mental attitude, you can achieve great things in life. I had bought what they were selling, lock, stock, and barrel, and it had paid off far greater than I could have imagined — at least on paper.

I didn't realize it at the time, but it was an incomplete theology, a half-truth, that led me to seek salvation and redemption through wealth. I had grown to love money. It became my god, a false god that left me standing at the altar of life, empty-handed and broken-hearted. Now I served a new master. If the gospel of Jesus Christ wasn't true, it meant nothing, but if it was true, nothing was more important.

As I approached Lise with the financial statements, hands shaking, I asked her to join me in prayer. Kneeling with our heads bowed, I clutched the papers in one hand and her hand in the other. As I prayed, my voice, soft and serious, cracked. "God, you are our God, the one and only God, the ruler of the universe. We are going home tomorrow. We want to serve you with all of our hearts and all of our souls. We want to do your will, not ours. We don't want these earthly riches to distract us from following you. All that we have and all that we are belongs to you."

One year earlier, we had surrendered our lives to Christ, but I still hadn't surrendered our finances. They had become my fortress, a refuge from an indifferent world. Finally, for the first time ever, I was surrendering it all. Everything I held sacred was put on the altar as an offering to God.

Tears filling my eyes, I continued through fearful sobs. "God, we surrender our finances to you. They are yours, not ours. If you want us to give it all away today, just tell us, and we will. We will walk out of this room penniless and follow you forever. Show us; tell us what you want us to do. We are yours."

On our knees with our heads bowed, we held hands in solemn silence, listening, waiting, and trusting that God would show us the way.

Chapter 26
Home Again

The midday sun warmed my face, and the smell of freshly cut grass tickled my nose. The only sounds were the breeze blowing through our giant evergreen trees and the robins chirping as they pecked around Lise's untended vegetable garden. My country girl would be stomping around in her muddy boots and nursing that patch of dirt back to life soon enough.

Home again with my company sold, I was free from the headaches of managing 500 employees and the risks and responsibilities of running a large organization. I had spent the first half of my life living for all the wrong things. I wanted the second half to count. Where to go and what to do wasn't clear, but I had faith that God would show me the way.

* * * * *

A few months later, I was sitting in the quiet comfort of Montreal's historic Queen Elizabeth Hotel dining room eating my bacon and eggs Benny — medium, poached — as I watched the morning rush-hour traffic inch by and people scurry down busy sidewalks to work. As inner-city kids, my friends and I had gotten into a lot of mischief here. These streets and subways had been our playground. Thirty-five years later, my life had come full circle. Now I was one of those mysterious people on the inside looking out, seemingly above the hustle and bustle of everyday life.

My journey back to Montreal had begun a year earlier when my friend Nigel had submitted the Vivian as a candidate for the Kaufman Foundation's Community Service Award. The foundation is the legacy of Ewing Marion Kauffman, an American entrepreneur and philanthropist who believed in the value of entrepreneurship and education. Much to our surprise, we won.

Coincidentally, this year's presentation was being made at the EO conference in my hometown of Montreal. The conference, called a "University," is a four-day event where some of the world's greatest business and thought leaders come together with young, ambitious entrepreneurs.

On the morning of the award ceremony, the hotel ballroom was filled with hundreds of my peers from around the world. I was anxious as a lifetime of insecurity and self-doubt welled up inside. *I don't belong here,* I thought. *I'm just a street-smart guy from the other side of the tracks. All of these college-educated middle-class people can't relate to my life. They don't care about me, my mother, or the work at the Vivian.* As this negative voice grew louder, I prayed silently until the time came to take the stage with Lise, Donavon, and Jasmine.

After acknowledging the great work being done by the other contestants, the presenter played a five-minute video that the Foundation had produced about the Vivian. The stark reality of our work and my mother's story must have made a powerful impression, because when the video ended, the audience rose to their feet and gave us a roaring standing ovation.

Together on stage under the bright lights in that beautiful ballroom, we watched as our story moved a sea of people to their feet and to tears. Little did they realize they had collectively silenced the lies and whispers that had sought to discourage and control me for most of my life.

David Ash

Chapter 27
The Little Warriors

"People brought little children to Jesus for him to place his
hands on them and pray for them. But the disciples rebuked
them. Jesus said, 'Let the little children come to me, and do
not hinder them, for the kingdom of heaven belongs to such
as these.' "
—Matthew 19: 13–14, *NIV*

Her voice exploded through the phone. "The work you are
doing at the Vivian is incredible! As I sat there watching
the video, I lost it. I was crying. I couldn't help myself. I was
sexually abused as a child. Because of that, I've dealt with
depression and anxiety all my life." The lady paused, gasping
for breath to power her next words. "I've always wanted to do
something, but I didn't know where to start. When you spoke
at the conference, I was given a vision and the name for an
organization that I'm going to start to help victims of sexual
abuse. Thank you for sharing your incredible story and inspiring me."

The woman on the phone was Glori, a fellow EO member
from Edmonton. She had called me a few days after I returned
home from the conference. I had never been thanked and
encouraged so much by an absolute stranger. At the end of

the call, I thanked her for her kind words, encouraged her to follow her dreams, and then jumped back into by busy life without giving the call a second thought.

＊　＊　＊　＊　＊

As I scanned the online news story, a smile came across my face. I had Googled myself one afternoon five years after that unexpected telephone call and noticed numerous links connecting my name with an organization called the Little Warriors. That high-energy lady on the phone had made good on her promise. I had to give her a call.

Two weeks later, we huddled around a small table in a cozy little Italian restaurant on a cold winter's night, the smell of warm bread and delicious pasta filling the air. The happy murmur of our fellow patrons savoring their week's reward forced me to lean in close to hear what Glori and her husband Gary were saying. I had come to Edmonton to hear their incredible story firsthand. As we talked, I felt an immediate connection, a comfort level I only ever experience with close personal friends. Soon, I discovered that Glori has that effect on a lot of people.

Glori told me she had grown up in a single-parent, father-absent home. Under financial pressure, her mother was forced to move back in with her parents, who cared for Glori while she worked. What no one knew at that time was that her grandfather was a pedophile, and he secretly abused her for years.

Glori had struggled with emotional problems due to her abuse for her entire life. In her search for help, she was surprised by the lack of specialized programs and therapy. She wanted to do something for others but didn't know where to start — until that fateful day in Montreal.

"As I watched the Vivian video, I had a supernatural download from God," Glori said, excitement in her eyes. "The Little Warriors name and a plan became perfectly clear to me. I was bawling my eyes out as I scribbled down the ideas that flooded my mind." Glori went on to explain how she transformed her vision into a reality.

Today, Little Warriors is Canada's single largest resource for the victims of sexual abuse. They have developed cutting-edge prevention and awareness programs that reach thousands of people each year. Glori and Gary also own an advertising agency, g[squared], and use their industry influence to secure millions of dollars in free advertising for Little Warriors annually. Whenever the media asks Glori for the source of her inspiration, she credits my story and the Vivian, which explains the online articles linked to my name.

All of this has come at great personal cost to Glori and her family. When we were together, she confessed that her work had taken a toll. Depression, anxiety, and panic attacks had made regular life impossible. Unable to run from her past any longer, she was forced to seek counseling. It was this therapy that gave her the courage and strength to confront her abuser for the first time. When she did, she was devastated by her family's response. Some refused to believe her, while others wanted to sweep the matter under the rug. Surprisingly, this type of familial denial is not the exception but the rule, which is why so many victims of sexual abuse are unable to come to peace with their past. In Glori's case, her grandfather was criminally charged and convicted of his crimes. He died a few years later.

When I met Glori that night, she also shared a much larger dream. Through their advocacy and prevention programs, she had discovered a huge crack in the system. Many victims needed a safe place to go, far away from the people who had hurt them, so they could heal, but there was no such place in all of Canada. Glori was determined to change that. She had a vision for a residential treatment center, a ranch, where kids could receive 24/7 care and support from highly trained professionals. All she needed was funding and a ranch.

As I sat back and listened to her story, I reflected on our work with the mentally ill, addicted, and homeless on Vancouver's Downtown East Side. It was emotionally and financially draining. Progress occurred at glacial speed. The wins were few, the losses great, and people died all the time. We had stood by and watched passionate frontline workers and friends burn out, and we saw their families fall apart. In those dark hours, when I felt like throwing in the towel, I found myself on my knees crying out to God and asking him if what we were doing was making any difference. His answer was always the same: "I love these people as much as I loved your mother. Love them for me."

Glori's story was an encouraging answer to those same desperate prayers. We were making a difference, in ways that we could never imagine or would ever know about. It was a reminder that "what is impossible with man is possible with God" (Luke 18:27, *NIV*).

* * * * *

The more I thought about Glori and the seemingly unconnected chain of events that had brought us together, the more I thought about Mike, the entrepreneur who had inspired me with his company's giving program when he spoke about it during our Birthing of Giants class eight years earlier. I hadn't seen or talked to him since, but I wanted him to know how his story had changed my life and the lives of countless others. On November 1, 2011, I tracked down his address and sent him the following e-mail.

David Ash

Mike,

You may not remember me, but I haven't forgotten you. We were BOG classmates, and you shared something one day that changed my life.

It was the class on "giving back" that struck me so profoundly. It came at a time in my business career when I had turned the corner financially in a big way. I was overwhelmed with adjusting to my new financial reality. You were the first person I had ever met who was engaged in such committed generosity within your company. When you shared your story, my jaw dropped. I come from a blue-collar family from the "other side of the tracks." If I saw someone profiled in the media who was supposedly amazingly generous, my cynical mind and hard heart would explain it away. Your story was the first real evidence of significant selfless generosity I had ever witnessed personally. You truly inspired me. It gave me a sense of meaning and purpose for my newfound wealth.

I left class that year committed to being more deliberate in my giving. As a result, I became a supporter of numerous organizations that provide food, shelter, and other services for the homeless and the mentally ill in Canada. One of the projects we initiated and funded is a 24-bed rooming house for hard to house women called The Vivian. It was named after my mother, who suffered from mental illness and eventually died alone as a street person. A short video at www.thedagroup.ca explains more. This video was produced free for us by the Kaufman Foundation, an EO sponsor. We received the Kauffman Foundation's Community Award in 2005. Without my knowledge Nigel, a Forum group buddy, submitted the project for consideration. When they played the video and I received the award at the Montreal EO University, I was overwhelmed by the emotional response I received. There was a standing ovation and many tears.

When I returned home, an Edmonton EO member, Glori Meldrum called me. She said she was deeply moved by my message and cried throughout the presentation. She also said she was inspired to start an organization that would help children who are sexually abused. She was a victim herself. I thanked her for her kind words, encouraged her, and thought little more about it.

A year ago I discovered that Glori made good on her commitment and started an amazing organization called Little Warriors (www.littlewarriors.ca). They train over 500 people each month on how to recognize, prevent, and counsel people to deal with sexually abused children. I met Glori and her husband Gary for the first time last week. Great people.

In retrospect, your testimony of radical kindness and generosity in class that day sparked my own spiritual journey. This led to my eventual faith in Jesus Christ in 2003. The greatest decision of my entire life. I have, in every sense of the word, been born again. I am a new man.

I wanted you to know the exponential, generational impact your story had that day. You sharing your story of goodness and generosity, in humility, changed my life, the life of my wife, my children, and my children's children forever. Your story has also changed Glori's life and the lives of the thousands of vulnerable children that Little Warriors helps every year. We will never know the full impact. Thank you for your obedience to God's call on your life.

David

When I opened my inbox later that day and saw Mike's response, my heart skipped a beat.

Wow... I'm sitting here praying no one wanders by my desk and wonders why I have tears streaming down my face.

What a crazy cool story and a crazy neat thing you are doing.

It's an encouragement to me more than you can imagine.

I guess the church is supposed to be like this, where we all chip in a little bit of what we are learning, then the Holy Spirit grabs hold and starts doing some wild cool stuff ... but when it happens, it still gives goose bumps, tears, and chills, and sadly I'm surprised at some level.

I'm just glad we crossed paths back then and had a chance to share some thoughts on using business as a tool to make a difference in the world ... and now you get to apply it in the context of a relationship with Christ!

Mike hadn't changed. His kind words conveyed the same spirit that had inspired me eight years earlier. I looked forward to the day that our paths would cross again.

Chapter 28
Be Brave

Last year, Glori's dream came true.

On a cold but sunny September afternoon, Lise and I were honored guests at the grand opening ceremony of the Little Warriors Be Brave Ranch. The 60,000-square-foot facility perched on 120 acres of beautiful Alberta ranchland looked a lot like a high-end summer camp. Hundreds of friends and supporters were in attendance, along with the media, local politicians, and dignitaries. Theo Fleury, retired NHL hockey player and sexual abuse survivor, spoke glowingly about Glori and Little Warriors. A band played, faces were painted, and hot dogs were eaten. A grand time was had by all.

As I watched hundreds of people milling joyfully about the ranch and Glori buzzing from person to person, hugging, thanking, and celebrating, I couldn't help but grin inwardly as I thought about how happy my mother would be to know that her tragic life story had inspired an organization that would bring healing to thousands of children and save them from a fate similar to her own.

My mother, born with syphilis to a prostitute in the slums of Montreal, had been a Little Warrior herself. Unadoptable and a ward of the court, she fought for survival every day of her life until she died alone in that rooming house.

In an interesting twist of fate, my mother's fighting spirit had earned her the moniker "The Warrior Vendor" on the streets of Halifax, where she sold *Street Feat,* an anti-poverty magazine. We also discovered that she was a poet and contributor to *Street Feat* under the pen name "A Warrior." Her poem "My Life" is my favorite:

My Life

Please judge us not but give us hope,
To rise above our pain and despair.
Take action to help us fight our fight
And change our plight and know someday
We will win against the pain we feel within.
Our hope returns, our dreams come true.
Our pain will turn to joy once more
And we will fight the fight for all who came before.
Those like me will overcome our foe
And those who fight along with us
Will never let our circle be broken.
Alpha-Omega.
We will win the fight.
Of this fact I know.
~ A Warrior ~

I read this poem, and several others like it, for the first time at my mother's memorial service in Halifax, Nova Scotia. Emotionally overwhelmed, I was unable to see anything other than the ramblings of a mad women, living alone on the margins of society. The "Alpha-Omega" reference meant nothing to me. Since then, however, I've learned that alpha and omega are the first and last letters of the Greek alphabet as well as a reference to God in the Book of Revelation: " 'I am the Alpha and the Omega,' says the Lord God, who is, and who was, and who is to come, the Almighty" (Revelation 1:8, *NIV*).

When I read her poem again with this scriptural reference in mind, I heard the voice of a modern-day psalmist, boldly proclaiming her faith in a God who loves widows, orphans, and Little Warriors:

> [With the] Alpha [and the] Omega,
> [The Lord God, who is, and who was,
> And who is to come, the Almighty,]
> We will win the fight.
> Of this fact I know.
> ~ A Warrior ~

Chapter 29
Life Goes On

"And the peace of God, which transcends all understanding,
will guard your hearts and minds in Christ Jesus."
—Philippians 4:7, *NIV*

Cape Town is South Africa's top tourist destination. Hundreds of thousands of visitors flock there every year to enjoy its beaches and watch the Indian and Atlantic oceans splash together off its shores. One of the main tourist attractions is Robben Island, the notorious prison that held Nelson Mandela for 18 of the 27 years he was in jail.

There is another side of Cape Town that few visitors see: the Masiphumelele Township, or Masi. This community is home to 38,000 people, all living well below the poverty line. Eighty-five percent of the homes here are dirt-floor shacks made from corrugated sheet metal and scrap lumber. Twenty-three percent of the population is infected with HIV/AIDS, and 89 percent of the residents are black, not "colored" — a sad but important distinction to residents in post-apartheid South Africa.

A little over a year after returning home from our YWAM DTS, my family and I found ourselves in Masi with our new YWAM friends doing repairs and upgrades to some of the shacks. The days were long and the sun was hot as Donavon, Jasmine, Lise, and I worked together, doing the best we could with what we had to offer. At night we would gather around the dinner table, sunburnt, tired, and fresh from hot showers, glad to be wearing clean clothes again.

As we ate, we chatted about our days, laughing and sharing stories of our adventures. While the poverty we confronted was disturbing and our hearts broke for the people we helped, we all felt a supernatural joy and peace in the midst of these acts of selflessness. It was the same deep, comforting Spirit that we had felt when we renovated the Vivian and built homes for the poor in Mexico together. It was a peace that "transcended all understanding."

After selling my business, I spent a lot of time praying about what to do next. I yearned to serve God in any way that I could. *How?* was the question. It quickly became clear that I wasn't wired to be a full-time pastor or missionary in the traditional sense. All of us are created uniquely and powerfully in the image of God, and there is no doubt that God wired me to be an entrepreneur. While I may have misused the gifts and talents he gave me in the past, I realized that they were his gifts nonetheless, and for me to reject them would be tantamount to rejecting God himself.

Today, I operate in God's economy. I no longer measure my success in dollars and cents. My time, talents, and financial resources are focused on achieving God's purposes instead of my own. Feeding the hungry, clothing the naked, caring for widows and orphans, and loving my neighbor, wherever I meet him or her, are my priorities.

Over the last 13 years, we've had the honor and pleasure of meeting and partnering with men and women from all walks of life and every corner of the earth. These unsung heroes have given up everything for the cause of Christ. We've been to Africa, China, India, Cambodia, Southeast Asia, and

North Korea; in the slums, in orphanages, in schools, and in marketplaces. We don't always speak the same language, but we know each other's hearts instantly, because we share the same spirit — the Holy Spirit — which is alive in all of us, everywhere, all at once.

Of course, living this life out faithfully hasn't always been easy. I am far from perfect, and as my pastor, Doug, always reminds us, "Life is messy." Thankfully, "God's mercies are new every morning" (Lam 3:22–23, *NLT*), and when I fall short, he convicts, forgives, comforts, and encourages me to try again.

Writing this book has been a labor of love. The love of an all-powerful, almighty God, that helped me make sense of a world that had made no sense at all. I came to God empty-handed and broken-hearted, and he took me as I was. If he hasn't already, he will take you, too.

Bad credit? No credit? No problem!